A SHORT COURSE IN
USING YOUR DIGITAL CAMERA
A GUIDE TO GREAT PHOTOGRAPHS

FOURTH EDITION

DENNIS P. CURTIN

SHORTCOURSES.COM
HTTP://WWW.SHORTCOURSES.COM

SHORT COURSES PUBLISHING PROGRAM

Short Courses is the leading publisher of digital photography books, textbooks, and guides to specific cameras from Canon, Sony, Nikon, Olympus and others. All of these books are available on-line from the Short Courses bookstore at:

http://www.shortcourses.com/bookstore/book.htm

All recent books are available in both black & white printed and full-color eBook (PDF) versions. The list of books we've published is rapidly expanding so be sure to visit the store to see if there is a book on your camera.

If you find any errors in this book, would like to make suggestions for improvements, or just want to let me know what you think—I welcome your feedback.

ShortCourses.com
16 Preston Beach Road
Marblehead, Massachusetts 01945
E-mail: denny@shortcourses.com
Web site: http://www.shortcourses.com

To learn more about digital photography visit our two Web sites:

■ http://www.shortcourses.com is our consumer site.
■ http://www.photocourse.com is our instructor/student site.

EDUCATORS

This has always been a popular text in digital photography courses. If you are an instructor or student, you should know that special pricing is available for classroom use.

For details on using this and other texts in the classroom, please visit our education site at www.photocourse.com.

ISBN 1-928873-67-7

THE eBOOK EDITION AND MULTIMEDIA

The eBook version of this book includes clickable links that display animations and other resources stored on the PhotoCourse.com Web site. To view them you need an Internet connection. These animations and other resources are designed to help you understand the basic concepts of digital photography so it's easier for you to master your camera and its controls. If you have the eBook version, just click any button that looks like the one to the left. The animation that is played is related to the digital photography concept discussed on that page.

The multimedia elements on the eBook version of this book were originally developed for our new book *"Photo Course—An Interactive Multimedia eText."* If you find that they enhance your understanding of digital photography you may want to see more. Click the CD below to learn more about this exciting new 300 page introduction to digital photography.

If you like the printed version of this book, you may want to get a copy of the eBook version or a copy of our new book Photo Course —An Interactive Multimedia eText *with over 300 pages and 90 animations and other resources on digital photography. Click the CD disc to learn more.*

Adobe's Acrobat Reader displays tabs on the left side of the page. Clicking the Bookmarks *tab displays a table of contents and clicking the* Pages *tab displays thumbnails of each page.*

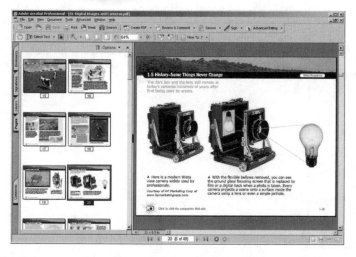

PREFACE

The virtue of the camera is not the power it has to transform the photo-grapher into an artist, but the impulse it gives him to keep on looking— and looking. (Brooks Atkinson, Once Around the Sun).

PHOTOGRAPHY ON-LINE

The contents of this book are constantly updated, enhanced, and expanded on-line. To learn more about digital photography, visit our Short-Courses Web site at www.short-courses.com.

A great photograph begins when you recognize a great scene or subject. But recognizing a great opportunity isn't enough to capture it; you also have to be prepared. A large part of being prepared involves understanding your camera well enough to capture what you see the way you want to interpret it. Getting you prepared to see and capture great photographs is what this book is all about. It doesn't matter if you are taking pictures for business or pleasure, there's a lot here to help you get better results and more satisfaction from your photography.

To get better, and possibly even great photographs, you need to understand both concepts and procedures; the "whys" and "hows" of photography.

■ Concepts of photography are the underlying principles that apply regardless of the camera you are using. They include such things as how sharpness and exposure affect your images and the way they are perceived by viewers. Understanding concepts answers the "why" kinds of questions you might have about photography.

■ Procedures are those things specific to one kind of camera, and explain step-by-step how you set your camera's controls to capture an image just the way you want to. Understanding procedures gives you the answers to the "how" kinds of questions you might have.

This book is organized around the concepts of digital photography because that's how photographers think. You think about scenes and subjects, highlights and shadows, softness and sharpness, color and tone. Discussions of the procedures you use with some or all cameras are integrated throughout the concepts in places where they apply. This integrated approach lets you first understand the concepts of photography and then see where to look in your camera manual for the specific steps you use in all kinds of photographic situations. There are even places for you to write in notes about how you do it with your own camera.

To get more effective, interesting, and creative photographs, you only need to understand how and when to use a few simple features on your camera such as focus, exposure controls, and flash. If you've previously avoided understanding these features and the profound impact they can have on your images, you'll be pleased to know that you can learn them on a weekend. You can then spend the rest of your life marveling at how the infinite variety of combinations they provide make it possible to convey your own personal view of the world. You'll be ready to keep everything in a scene sharp for maximum detail or to blur it all for an impressionistic portrayal. You'll be able to get dramatic close-ups, freeze fast action, create wonderful panoramas, and capture the beauty and wonder of rainbows, sunsets, fireworks, and nighttime scenes.

As you explore your camera, be sure to have fun. There are no "rules" or "best" way to make a picture. Great photographs come from using what you know to experiment and try new approaches. Digital cameras make this especially easy because there are no film costs or delays. Every experiment is free and you see the results immediately so you can learn step by step.

CONTENTS

Chapter 1
Camera Controls & Creativity

CONTENTS

Serious digital cameras give you creative control over your images. They do so by allowing you to control the light and motion in photographs as well as what's sharp and what isn't. Although most consumer digital cameras are fully automatic, some allow you to make minor adjustments that affect your images. Many cameras, including high-end point and shoots and digital SLRs, offer a wide range of controls. However, regardless of what controls your camera has, the same basic principles are at work "under the hood." Your automatic exposure and focusing systems are having a profound effect on your images. However, even with your camera on automatic mode, you can indirectly control, or at least take advantage of the effects these systems have on your images.

In this chapter, we'll first explore how you use the camera in various automatic modes and see what effect each of the settings has on your images. In the chapters that follow, we'll explore in greater depth how you take control of these settings, and others, to get the effects that you want.

TAKING PHOTOS IN AUTOMATIC MODE

HOW TO: SELECTING AUTOMATIC MODE

Look in your camera manual for a section on selecting *auto* or *automatic exposure mode*:

_____

_____

_____

All digital cameras have an automatic mode that sets focus and exposure for you. All you have to do is frame the image and push the shutter button. You'll find that this auto mode of operation is great in the vast majority of situations because it lets you focus on the subject and not on the camera. Here's a brief guide to using auto mode on almost any camera.

■ **Getting ready**. Turn the camera on and set it to automatic mode—usually spelled out or indicated by a camera icon. To conserve your batteries, turn off the monitor and compose your image through the optical viewfinder if your camera has one. (Digital SLR cameras don't let you compose the image on the monitor and some point and shoots don't have optical viewfinders.) If the camera has a lens cap, be sure to remove it.

■ **Framing the image**. The viewfinder or monitor shows you the scene you are going to capture. To zoom the lens to frame your image, press the zoom-out button or lever to widen the angle of view and the zoom-in button or lever to enlarge subjects. If using an SLR, you zoom by turning a ring on the lens. If the image in the viewfinder is fuzzy, see if the camera has a diopter adjustment you can use to sharpen it.

HOW TO: TURNING THE MONITOR ON AND OFF

Look in your camera manual for a section on *LCD monitor*:

_____

_____

_____

_____

■ **Autofocus**. Cameras have one or more focus zones or areas, each of which is often indicated in the viewfinder with cross hairs, boxes or brackets. The part of the scene that you cover with one of these focus zones will be the sharpest part of the photo. Many cameras will focus on the center of the scene but others will focus on the closest part of the scene covered by any of the focus zones. How close you can focus depends on the camera and lens.

■ **Autoexposure**. The camera's exposure system measures light reflecting from the scene and uses these readings to set the best possible exposure.

■ **Autoflash**. If the light is too dim, the autoexposure system will fire the camera's built-in flash to illuminate the scene. If the flash is going to fire, a flash lamp usually glows when you press the shutter button halfway down.

■ **Automatic white balance**. Because the color in a photograph is affected by the color of the light illuminating the scene, a camera automatically adjusts white balance so white objects in a scene are white in the photo and other colors are free of a color cast.

READY OR NOT

On many cameras you can tell if the camera is ready to take a photo by pressing the shutter button halfway down. When you do so, lamps in or next to the viewfinder may glow to indicate when focus is set and the flash is ready to fire.

HOW TO: TAKING A PICTURE IN AUTOMATIC MODE

1. Turn the camera on and set it to automatic mode. Be sure to remove the lens cap.
2. Compose the image in the viewfinder or on the monitor, making sure the subject that you want sharpest is covered by the focus area used to set focus. If unsure, center it in the viewfinder.
3. Press the shutter button halfway down so the camera can set focus and exposure. When the camera has done so, a lamp may glow or the camera may beep.
4. Press the shutter button all the way down to take the picture. When you do so, the camera may beep. The camera then saves the new image onto the camera's memory card.
5. When done, turn the camera off.

GOOD THINGS TO KNOW

When you first start taking photos, it sometimes seems that there is too much to learn all at once. Here are some things you may want to know right off.

■ **The first time you use the camera**, or if the batteries have been removed or dead for an extended period, you should enter the date and time. The date and time will help you organize, locate, and identify your images later.

■ **Always check camera settings** on the control panel and in the viewfinder. Notice how many pictures you can take at the current settings and the status of the battery charge. Also, learn what the icons mean because it's not at all unusual to change a setting, then forget you have done so.

■ **If an image is being stored when you turn the camera off**, the image will be completely stored before the camera powers down.

■ **Most shutter buttons have two stages**. When you press it halfway down, the camera sets focus and exposure. When you press it all the way down, you take the picture. To capture action shots, hold the button halfway down while focused on the scene. When you then press the button the rest of the way, the camera shoots immediately because focus and exposure have already been calculated. On some cameras you can also press the shutter button all the way down in one action, but there will be a delay before the photo is taken and it may be out of focus.

■ **If the viewfinder appears blurry**, see if the camera has an diopter adjustment that makes it sharper.

■ **To take pictures**, hold the camera in your right hand and support the camera or lens with your left. Don't block the flash, autofocus port, or lens.

■ **As you take photos**, they are first stored in the camera's internal memory called a "buffer." When the buffer is full you'll have to wait until one or more of the images has been transferred to the memory card before taking any more pictures.

■ **Don't open the battery or memory card access covers** while an image is being saved. Doing so can not only damage the image being saved, it can also damage the card.

■ **Some cameras will briefly display the image** you just took as it is being saved. Usually you can turn this feature on or off.

■ **You can usually adjust the brightness of the monitor**. Make it brighter in bright light and dimmer in dim light.

■ **Many cameras have a tripod socket** so you can attach it to a tripod when you want sharper pictures.

■ **Take as many shots of a given scene as you can think of**; changing positions, distances, and angles. You may be surprised later at what works and what doesn't.

■ **When done shooting**, turn the camera off.

Most shutter buttons have two stages.

Most cameras store images on a removable memory card that slides into a slot on the camera. Courtesy of Kodak.

WHEN THINGS GO WRONG

Icons on the camera's control panel or monitor indicate the status of the batteries. The icons, many of which look like these, show when the battery is fully charged (left) and getting low (right).

If anything can go wrong, it will. Here are some of the things you might encounter.

■ **If the camera seem to be turned off**, it may just have entered sleep mode. If you don't use any controls for a specified time, the camera enters this mode to reduce battery drain. To wake it up, press the shutter button halfway down, or turn the camera off and back on. After an hour or so of inactivity, some cameras shut off completely. You can often change the time it takes before the camera enters sleep mode or turns off completely.

■ **If you can't turn on the camera**, the batteries are dead or have been removed or a memory card hasn't been inserted.

■ **If your batteries drain quickly**, stop using the monitor to take and review pictures. If it's cold, keep the batteries or camera under your coat.

■ **When you turn the camera on**, a battery shaped icon on the control panel indicates when the batteries are fully charged, getting low, or run down empty and should be replaced immediately.

■ **When you turn on the camera**, an error message will be displayed if there is a problem with the memory card.

■ **If you can't take a picture**, it may be because the memory card is full. To free up room for new pictures, move the images to a computer and erase the memory card, delete some you don't need, or switch to a smaller image size.

■ **Some cameras have a delay** between your pressing the shutter button and the shutter opening. This can cause you to miss fleeting expressions.

■ **To control which part of the scene the camera focuses on**, read your user guide so you understand how focus works in various exposure modes.

■ **If the focus lamp blinks** when you press the shutter button halfway down, the camera may be having trouble focusing.

■ **If the flash lamp blinks** when you press the shutter button halfway down, the flash is charging. Release the shutter button for a few seconds and try again.

■ **If flash photos are too dark**, you are probably too far from the subject. Most built-in flash units are good only up to about ten feet. They don't have the power to illuminate subjects much father than that.

■ **If photos are too light when using flash**, you may want to reduce the flash power.

■ **If your pictures are blurred**, you may not be holding the camera steady as you smoothly press the shutter. Most blurry photos are caused by jabbing the shutter button. You may also be too close to the subject or the subject may be moving too fast.

■ **Never take pictures of the sun or other bright light sources**. Doing so can injure your eye or the camera's image sensor.

■ **If your pictures are not at all the way you expect**, it may be because the camera remembered a change you made in the settings and continues to use that changed setting. Some cameras remember changes even when you turn a camera off and back on. See if your camera has a procedure that resets all settings to their factory defaults.

When deleting files or formatting memory cards, think before you do so. It's easy to loose files.

TYPES OF DIGITAL CAMERAS

When it comes time to choose a new digital camera, there is quite a range of types to choose among. You are usually trading off size versus flexibility. Pocket sized cameras usually don't have all of the features of larger cameras, but they are much more convenient. The best news is that despite their great differences, most cameras will capture very good image quality, especially when used to create snapshot-sized prints.

This old Kodak ad slogan now applies to the entire field of digital photography. With kiosks everywhere, it's easy to shoot and then just print the images you want.

Point and shoot cameras usually have fewer controls than other digital cameras but many are also small, bordering on tiny. With a camera that fits into your pocket, you're more likely to have it when you need it.

Camera phone quality is improving rapidly with 8 megapixel models already available in some parts of the world. In time these cameras may present real competition to point and shoot cameras.

The fastest selling point and shoot digital cameras are those built into camera phones. The problem with these cameras is that their image quality is improving very slowly and doesn't yet match that of dedicated cameras.

One-time-use cameras take surprisingly good pictures and some even have a monitor on which you can review your results.

Digital photography has already matured to the point where there are one-time-use point and shoot versions.

Fixed lens cameras often have great zoom lenses and capture large images.

Pentax makes underwater cameras including the Optio WPi.

High-end fixed lens cameras usually have a zoom lens and many of the exposure and focus controls found on SLR cameras.

Single-lens reflex cameras (SLRs) are the most flexible and often the most expensive cameras.

SLR cameras from major companies have more lenses than you'll ever need.

DIRTY SECRET

■ Removing the lens from an SLR lets dust enter the camera and settle on the sensor. This dust creates dark spots in your images. You can remove the dust yourself but it's risky (page 123).

One of the most popular camera types among professionals and serious amateurs is the single-lens reflex, better known as an SLR. These cameras are expensive but have certain advantages over other camera types:

■ You can change lenses.

■ You see the scene through the lens so what you see is what you get. (Fixed lens cameras with electronic viewfinders differ from SLRs in that they don't use a movable mirror to bounce light into the viewfinder.)

■ You can select from a large variety of accessories, including powerful flash units.

UNDERSTANDING IMAGE SIZE AND QUALITY

Digital photographs are actually mosaics of millions of tiny squares called *picture elements*—or just *pixels*. Like the impressionists who painted wonderful scenes with small dabs of paint, your computer and printer can use these tiny pixels to display or print photographs. To do so, the computer divides the screen or printed page into a grid of pixels. It then uses the values stored in the digital photograph to specify the brightness and color of each pixel in this grid—a form of painting by number.

A digital image that looks sharp and has smooth transitions in tones (top) is actually made up of millions of individual square pixels (bottom). Each pixel is a solid, uniform color.

TIP

■ A few camera companies, even some that are otherwise respectable, try to deceive you into thinking their cameras have higher resolution than they really do. They use software to inflate the size of a captured image and then use this inflated size in advertising claims about the camera. This way each captured pixel can suddenly become four, and voila' a 2 megapixel image suddenly and magically becomes 8.

NUMBER OF PIXELS

The quality of a digital image depends in part on the number of pixels used to create the image (sometimes referred to as *resolution*). At a given size, more pixels add detail and sharpen edges. However, there are always size limits. When you enlarge any digital image enough, the pixels begin to show—an effect called *pixelization*. This is not unlike traditional silver-based prints where grain begins to show when prints are enlarged past a certain point.

The term "resolution" has two meanings in photography. Originally it referred to the ability of a camera system to resolve pairs of fine lines such as those found on a test chart. In this usage it's an indicator of sharpness, not image size. With the introduction of digital cameras the term began being used to indicate the number of pixels a camera could capture.

When a digital image is displayed or printed at the correct size for the number of pixels it contains, it looks like a normal photograph. When enlarged too much (as is the eye here), its square pixels begin to show.

The pixel size of a digital photograph is specified in one of two ways—by its dimensions in pixels or by the total number of pixels it contains. For example, the same image can be said to have 4368 × 2912 pixels (where "×" is pronounced "by" as in "4368 by 2912"), or to contain 12.7 million pixels or megapixels (4368 multiplied by 2912).

Image sizes are expressed as dimensions in pixels (4368 × 2912) or by the total number of pixels (12.7 megapixels).

TIP

■ Good prints can be made using 200 pixels per inch. Using this as a guide you can calculate that a 2000 x 1600 pixel image (just over 3 megapixels) will make a good 10 x 8 inch print.

An image sensor sits against a background enlargement of its square pixels, each capable of capturing one pixel in the final image. Courtesy of IBM.

The gray scale, seen best in black and white photos, contains a range of tones from pure black to pure white.

HOW TO: SE-
LECTING A
QUALITY MODE
Look in your
camera manual
for a section on
*image quality, im-
age size, compres-
sion, JPEG, TIFF,
or RAW.*

HOW AN IMAGE IS CAPTURED

Digital cameras are very much like earlier cameras. Beginning with the very first camera all have been basically black boxes with a lens, an aperture, and a shutter. The big difference between traditional film cameras and digital cameras is how they capture the image. Instead of film, digital cameras use a solid-state device called an *image sensor*. In some digital cameras the image sensor is a *charge-coupled device* (CCD), while in others it's a *CMOS sensor*. Both types can give very good results. On the surface of these fingernail-sized silicon chips are millions of photosensitive diodes, each of which captures a single pixel in the photograph to be.

When you take a picture the shutter opens briefly and each pixel on the image sensor records the brightness of the light that falls on it by accumulating an electrical charge. The more light that hits a pixel, the higher the charge it records. Pixels capturing light from highlights in the scene will have high charges. Those capturing light from shadows will have low charges.

After the shutter closes to end the exposure, the charge from each pixel is measured and converted into a digital number. This series of numbers is then used to reconstruct the image by setting the color and brightness of matching pixels on the screen or printed page.

IT'S ALL BLACK AND WHITE AFTER ALL

It may be surprising, but pixels on an image sensor only capture brightness, not color. They record the *gray scale*—a series of tones ranging from pure white to pure black. How the camera creates a color image from the brightness recorded by each pixel is an interesting story with its roots in the distant past.

When photography was first invented in the 1840s, it could only record black and white images. The search for color was a long and arduous process, and a lot of hand coloring went on in the interim (causing one photographer to comment "so you have to know how to paint after all!"). One major breakthrough was James Clerk Maxwell's 1860 discovery that color photographs could be created using black and white film and red, blue, and green filters. He had the photographer Thomas Sutton photograph a tartan ribbon three times, each time with a different color filter over the lens. The three black and white images were then projected onto a screen with three differ-

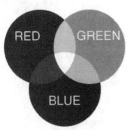

RGB uses just three basic colors to create full color images.

ent projectors, each equipped with the same color filter used to take the image being projected. When brought into alignment, the three images formed a full-color photograph. Over a century later, image sensors work much the same way.

Colors in a photographic image are usually based on the three primary colors red, green, and blue (RGB). This is called the *additive color system* because when the three colors are combined in equal amounts, they form white. This RGB system is used whenever light is projected to form colors as it is on the display monitor (or in your eye). Another color system uses cyan, magenta, yellow and black (CMYK) to create colors. This system is used in a few sensors and almost all printers since it's the color system used with reflected light.

Since daylight is made up of red, green, and blue light; placing red, green, and blue filters over individual pixels on the image sensor can create color images just as they did for Maxwell in 1860. Using a process called *interpolation*, the camera computes the actual color of each pixel by combining the color it captured directly through its own filter with the other two colors captured by the pixels around it. How well it does this is affected in part by the image format, size, and compression you select.

IMAGE FORMATS

One of the most important choices you'll make when shooting photos is what format to use—JPEG or RAW.

■ *JPEG* is the default format used by almost every digital camera ever made. Named after its developer, the Joint Photographic Experts Group (and pronounced "jay-peg") this format lets you specify both image size and compression. The smallest size is best for the Web and e-mail (although it will usually have to be reduced) and the largest for prints.

The JPEG format compresses images to make their files smaller, but many cameras let you specify how much they are compressed. This is a useful feature because there is a trade-off between compression and image quality. Less compression gives you better images so you can make larger prints, but you can't store as many images. Because you can squeeze more smaller or more compressed images onto a storage device, there may be times when you'll want to switch to the smaller size and sacrifice quality for quantity.

■ *RAW* images are often better than JPEG images because they are not processed in the camera, but on your more powerful desktop computer. These RAW files contain every bit of the captured data, unlike JPEGs which are always processed in the camera with some data being discarded. RAW files can be viewed, edited, and converted to other formats using most photo-editing software or programs included on a CD that comes with the camera. Some cameras let you capture RAW images by themselves or with a companion JPEG image that gives you an identical high quality RAW file and a smaller, more easily distributable JPEG image. When you use this feature, both the RAW and JPEG files have the same names but different extensions. The RAW format is discussed in more detail on page 62.

When you select an image format, size, and compression, you're not only affecting image quality but also how many images can be stored on your memory card. Sometimes when there is no storage space left, you can switch to a smaller size and higher compression to squeeze a few more images onto the card.

STORAGE CAPACITY

The number of new images you can store at the current settings is usually displayed on the camera's monitor or control panel.

EXPOSURE CONTROLS—THE SHUTTER AND APERTURE

One of the most important aspects of photography is getting the exposure right because it determines how light or dark an image is and what mood it conveys. The two most important exposure controls are the shutter speed and aperture because both affect the total amount of light reaching the image sensor. However, they do more than just control the exposure. As you'll see shortly they are also the most creative controls you have.

■ The *shutter* opens to begin an exposure and closes to end it. The shutter speed setting determines how long the shutter opens to expose the image sensor.

■ The *aperture* is the hole through which light enters the camera. The size of the hole can be changed to control the brightness of the light that reaches the image sensor.

If you strip away all of the modern technology and look at the earliest cameras, you will find the same controls in much simpler, and perhaps easier to understand, versions.

In the early days of photography, a plate called a waterhouse stop, **was inserted into a slot in the lens. The size of the stop's hole acted just like the iris apertures used today. A lens cap was removed and then replaced to begin and end the exposure—a primitive version of a shutter.**
This vintage camera is surrounded by waterhouse stops (apertures) and a lens cap (the shutter) leans against it.

Photo by Ake Borgstrom at www. photographica.nu.

Less light makes an image darker (left) and more light makes it lighter (right).

CHOOSING EXPOSURE MODES

Modes and how they are designated on the camera vary from model to model. Modes that give you the most control, available only on more advanced cameras, are usually indicated with letters. Those that are fully automatic, often called scene modes, are indicated with icons like those shown here on this Canon mode dial.

On some cameras you select exposure modes using buttons or a menu.

Modern digital cameras have sophisticated ways of controlling the aperture and shutter speed. In fully automatic mode the camera sets them both to produce the best possible exposure. However, there are other exposure modes that are widely used in digital photography. All modes give equally good results in the vast majority of photographic situations. However, when you photograph in specific kinds of situations, each of these exposure modes may have certain advantages. Let's take a look at the modes you can expect to find on some or all digital cameras.

■ Automatic mode sets the shutter speed and aperture without your intervention. This mode allows you to shoot without paying attention to settings so you can concentrate on composition and focus.

■ Scene modes have preselected settings for specific situations such as landscapes, portraits, night portraits, sports, and close-up photography.

■ Programmed mode is just like full auto in that it sets the aperture and shutter speed for you so you can concentrate on composition and action. When in this mode, many cameras have a flexible program mode that lets you select from a series of paired aperture and shutter speed combinations that yield the same exposure as that recommended by the camera but which give you control over depth of field and motion.

■ Shutter-priority mode lets you choose the shutter speed you need to freeze or deliberately blur camera or subject movement and the camera automatically sets the aperture to give you a good exposure. You select this mode when the portrayal of motion is most important. For example, when photographing action scenes, such as those encountered by wildlife photographers, sports photographers, and photojournalists, shutter-priority mode might be best. It lets you be sure your shutter speed is fast enough to freeze the action or slow enough to blur it

■ Aperture-priority mode lets you select the aperture needed to obtain the depth of field you want and the exposure system automatically sets the shutter speed to give you a good exposure. You select this mode whenever depth of field is most important. To be sure everything is sharp, as in a landscape, select a small aperture. The same holds true for close-up photography where depth of field is a major concern. To throw the background out of focus so it's less distracting in a portrait, select a large aperture.

■ Manual mode lets you select both the shutter speed and the aperture. You normally use this mode only when the other modes can't give you the results you want. Some cameras have a bulb setting in this mode that lets you capture time exposures such as light trails at night.

HOW TO: CHANGING EXPOSURE MODES

Look in your camera manual for sections on *automatic, scene,* or *program mode, aperture priority mode, shutter priority mode, shutter speeds,* and *apertures:*

_____

_____

_____

THE SHUTTER CONTROLS LIGHT AND MOTION

The shutter keeps light out of the camera except during an exposure, when it opens to let light strike the image sensor. In respect to just exposure, faster shutter speeds let less strike the image sensor so the image is darker. Slower speeds let in more so it's lighter.

As the shutter speed gets slower, the image gets lighter. The reason you don't usually see this effect in your images is because when you or the camera change the shutter speed, the camera changes the aperture to keep the exposure constant.

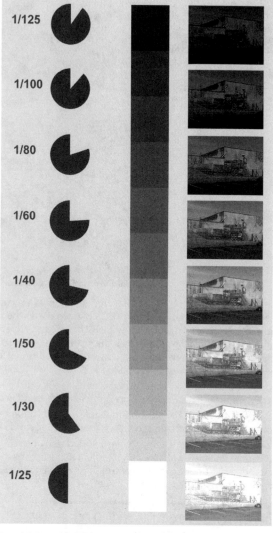

1/125

1/100

1/80

1/60

1/40

1/50

1/30

1/25

TIP

To get faster shutter speeds increase the ISO. To get slower shutter speeds, use a neutral density filter.

Katie turned a little just as the shutter opened causing unwanted blur in the image.

In addition to controlling exposure, the shutter speed is the most important control you have over how motion is captured in a photograph. The longer the shutter is open, the more a moving subject will be blurred in the picture Also, the longer it's open the more likely you are to cause blur by moving the camera slightly. Although you normally want to avoid blur in your images there are times when you may want to use it creatively.

A fast shutter speed (left) opens and closes the shutter so quickly a moving subject doesn't move very far during the exposure. A slow speed (right) can allow moving objects to move sufficiently to blur their image on the image sensor.

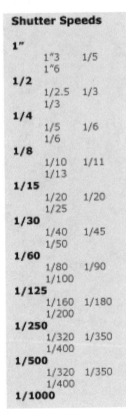

Shutter Speeds

1"		
	1"3	1/5
	1"6	
1/2		
	1/2.5	1/3
	1/3	
1/4		
	1/5	1/6
	1/6	
1/8		
	1/10	1/11
	1/13	
1/15		
	1/20	1/20
	1/25	
1/30		
	1/40	1/45
	1/50	
1/60		
	1/80	1/90
	1/100	
1/125		
	1/160	1/180
	1/200	
1/250		
	1/320	1/350
	1/400	
1/500		
	1/320	1/350
	1/400	
1/1000		

Although digital cameras can select any fraction of a second for an exposure, there are a series of settings that have traditionally been used when you set it yourself (which you can't do on many digital cameras). These shutter speed settings are arranged in a sequence so that each setting lets in half as much light as the next slowest setting and twice as much as the next fastest. Some of the traditional shutter speeds are listed to the left from the slowest to the fastest speeds.

■ Speeds faster than 1 second are fractions of a second and most cameras display them without the numerator. For example, 1/2 second is displayed as 2.

■ Speeds of 1 second or slower are whole seconds and many cameras indicate them with quotation or inch marks ("). For example, 2 seconds is displayed as 2".

Many high-end digital cameras have added one or two stops between each of the traditional ones. This allows you to adjust exposure in one-half or one-third stop increments for finer exposure control. In the table to the left one-third and one-half stops are shown in red and blue respectively.

HOW TO: SELECTING A SHUTTER SPEED
Look in your camera manual for a section on *shutter priority mode,* or *shutter speeds.*

THE APERTURE CONTROLS LIGHT AND DEPTH OF FIELD

The aperture adjusts the size of the opening through which light passes to the image sensor. The aperture can be opened up to let in more light or closed (stopped down) to let in less. In respect to just exposure, smaller apertures let less light strike the image sensor so the image is darker. Larger apertures let in more so it's lighter.

As the aperture number gets smaller (for example, from f/16 to f/11) the aperture opening gets larger and the image gets lighter. The reason you don't usually see this effect in your images is because when you or the camera change the aperture, the camera changes the shutter speed to keep the exposure constant.

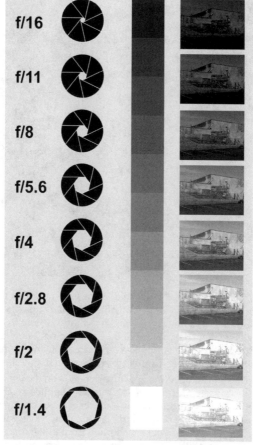

In better cameras, the aperture is a series of overlapping leaves located between the glass elements in the lens.

As with the shutter speed, the aperture also affects the sharpness of your picture, but in a different way. Changing the aperture changes the *depth of field*, the depth in a scene from foreground to background that will be sharp in a photograph. Smaller apertures increase depth of field while larger ones decrease it. For some pictures—for example, a landscape—you may want a smaller aperture for maximum depth of field so that everything from near foreground to distant background is sharp. But perhaps in a portrait you will want a larger aperture to decrease the depth of field so that your subject is sharp but the background is soft and out of focus.

Aperture settings are called *f-stops* and indicate the size of the aperture opening. Each f-stop lets in half as much light as the next larger opening and twice as much light as the next smaller opening. From the largest possible opening to increasingly smaller ones, the f-stops have traditionally been those shown to the left. No lens has the full range of settings; for example, the standard lens on a digital camera will range from

A small aperture increases depth of field so foreground and background are sharp (top) and a large aperture decreases depth of field so the background is soft (bottom).

TIP

To get smaller apertures increase the ISO. To get larger apertures, use a neutral density filter.

Apertures

f/1.4		
	f/1.6	f/1.7
	f/1.8	
f/2.0		
	f/2.2	f/2.5
	f/2.6	
f/2.8		
	f/3.2	f/3.4
	f/3.6	
f/4.0		
	f/4.5	f/4.7
	f/5.0	
f/5.6		
	f/6.3	f/6.7
	f/7.0	
f/8.0		
	f/9.0	f/9.5
	f/10	
f/11		
	f/13	f/13
	f/14	
f/16		

about f/2 to about f/16. Notice that as the f-stop number gets larger (f/8 to f/11, for example), the aperture size gets smaller. This may be easier to remember if you think of the f-number as a fraction: 1/11 is less than 1/8, just as the size of the f/11 lens opening is smaller that the size of the f/8 opening. Many high-end digital cameras have added one or two stops between each of the traditional ones. In the table to the left one-third and one-half stops are shown in red and blue respectively.

How wide you can open the aperture depends on the len's *maximum aperture*—its widest opening. The term "fast lens" usually applies to lenses that can be opened to a wide maximum aperture for the focal length. For example, a lens with a maximum aperture of f/1.8 opens wider, and is faster, than a lens with a maximum aperture of f/2.6. Faster lenses are better when photographing in dim light or photographing fast moving subjects. With most, but not all, zoom lenses the maximum aperture changes as you zoom the lens. It will be larger when zoomed out to a wide angle, and smaller when zoomed in to enlarge a subject.

HOW TO: SELECTING AN APERTURE
Look in your camera manual for a section on *aperture priority* or *apertures:*

_____

_____

_____

USING SHUTTER SPEED AND APERTURE TOGETHER

In this book and the animations apertures are represented by these realistic icons with a small aperture (left) and a large one (right).

In this book and the animations, shutter speeds are represented by these symbolic icons with a fast shutter speed (left) and a slow one (right). The cut out "pie slice" indicates how far an imaginary second hand would sweep.

On many cameras a quotation mark (") indicates full seconds and a fraction's denominator without a quotation mark indicates fractional seconds. For example, 2" means 2 seconds and 2 means 1/2 second.

When taking photos, one of the first decisions you make with many cameras is which exposure mode to use. As you've seen, your choice determines if you control the aperture or shutter speed. If your camera lets you select them, you can pair a fast shutter speed (to let in light for a short time) with a large aperture (to let in bright light) or a slow shutter speed (long time) with a small aperture (dim light).

Speaking of exposure only, it doesn't make any difference which combination you use. But in other ways, it does make a difference, and it is just this difference that gives you some creative opportunities. Whether you know it or not, you're always balancing camera or subject movement against depth of field because a change in one causes a change in the other. Let's see why.

As you've seen, shutter speeds and apertures each have a standard series of settings called "*stops.*"

■ With shutter speeds, each stop is a second or more, or a fraction of second indicating how long the shutter is open.

■ With apertures they are f/stops indicating the size of the opening through which light enters.

The stops are arranged so that a change of 1 stop lets in half or twice the light of the next setting. A shutter speed of 1/60 second lets in half the light that 1/30 second does, and twice the light of 1/125 second. An aperture of f/8 lets in half the light that f/5.6 does, and twice the light of f/11. If you make the shutter speed 1 stop slower (letting in 1 stop more light), and an aperture 1 full stop smaller (letting in 1 stop less light), the exposure doesn't change. (In all modes other than manual this happens automatically.) However, you increase the depth of field slightly and also the possibility of blur from camera or subject movement.

■ For fast-moving subjects you need a fast shutter speed (although the focal length of the lens you are using, the closeness of the subject, and the direction in which it's moving also affect how motion is portrayed). When photographing moving subjects shutter-priority mode is favored because it gives you direct control over the shutter speed.

■ For maximum depth of field, with the entire scene sharp from near to far, you need a small aperture (although the focal length of the lens and the distance to the subject also affects depth of field). When photographing landscapes and portraits aperture-priority mode is favored because it gives you direct control over the aperture and depth of field.

SHUTTER SPEED	READOUT
30 seconds	30"
4 seconds	4"
2 seconds	2"
1/2 second	2
1/4 second	4
1/30 second	30

EXPOSURE—FAUCETS & BUCKETS ANALOGY

One way to think of apertures and shutter speeds is to use the analogy of a faucet for the aperture and a timer for the shutter speed.

■ When you open a faucet all the way, water gushes out so you fill a bucket in a very short time. This is the same as pairing a large aperture and fast shutter speed to let in bright light for a short time.

■ When you open a faucet just a little, water trickles out and so it takes a much longer time to fill a bucket. This is the same as pairing a small aperture and slow shutter speed to let in dim light for a longer time.

No matter which combination you choose, the bucket is filled the same amount. Likewise, an image in a camera can be exposed the same amount by various aperture and shutter speed combinations while also controlling motion and depth of field.

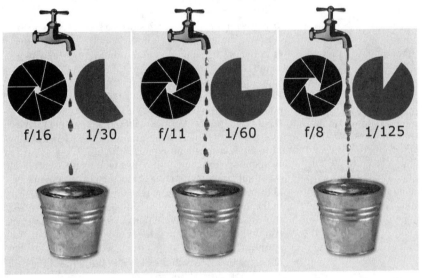

f/16   1/30   f/11   1/60   f/8   1/125

1. We start with the aperture set to f/16 and the shutter speed to 1/30.

2. When you open the aperture one stop to f/11 the shutter speed has to decrease to 1/60 to keep the exposure the same. This change decreases depth of field slightly and freezes action better.

3. When you open the aperture another stop to f/8 the shutter speed has to decrease another stop to 1/125. This change decreases depth of field even more and freezes action even better.

EXPOSURE—SEESAW ANALOGY

Another way to think of exposure is as a seesaw. As one child rises a given distance, the other falls by the same amount but their average distance from the ground is always the same. In photography, when you or the camera changes the aperture or shutter speed to let in more or less light, you or the camera must also change the other setting in the opposite direction to keep the exposure constant.

The illustrations below show how a change in the aperture setting must be matched by a change in the shutter speed and vice versa. As these offsetting changes are made, the exposure stays constant but depth of field changes slightly and subjects are more or less likely to be frozen.

1. Here the aperture is f/4 and the shutter speed is 1/125.

2. If you reduce the aperture one stop to f/5.6 the shutter speed has to decrease one stop to 1/60 to keep the exposure the same.

Depth of field increases slightly and the possibility of subject or camera blur increases.

3. If you reduce the aperture one more stop to f/8 the shutter speed has to decrease one more stop to 1/30 to keep the exposure the same.

Depth of field increases even more as does the possibility of subject or camera blur.

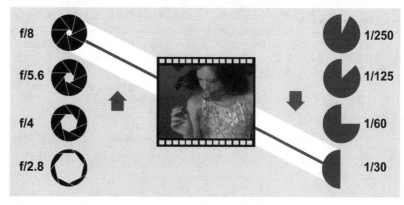

COMPOSING IMAGES

Monitors show you what the view looks like through the lens.

The best monitors are those that swivel and tilt to any angle.

With a swiveling monitor, you can shoot up at things close to the ground such as this newt.

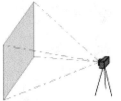

Landscape mode shows the image horizontally.

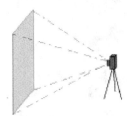

Portrait mode shows the image vertically.

To help you compose images, digital cameras usually have both a monitor and viewfinder. The primary roles of these two features are quite different, although there is some overlap.

MONITORS

Monitors are small LCD color displays built into most cameras. Their size is specified in inches, and the measurement, like those of TV sets, is based on the diagonal measurement. These screens range between 1.5 and 4 inches and serve a number of useful functions:

■ Menus are displayed on the monitor so you can change camera settings.

■ Image composition. On many, but not all cameras, you can compose the image on the screen before you take it. Most SLR cameras don't let you do this because they use a mirror to bounce the image formed by the lens into the viewfinder. The image sensor only creates the image when the shutter is open.

■ Image review. You can review an image you've taken so you know it's the way you want it. No more surprises as so often happens when you use a film camera and pick up your traditional prints.

■ Image management. You can scroll through the images you've taken and create slide shows, delete, rotate, rename, print, protect, copy or otherwise manage them. Many cameras also display thumbnails of a group of images in *index view* so you can quickly locate and select the images you're looking for. Most also let you enlarge the image on the monitor to zoom in on details in your photo—a great way to check sharpness. A few cameras let you view histograms of your image so you can check the tonal range. A few cameras now have touch-sensitive monitors so you can manage your images with a stylus instead of dials and buttons.

■ Direct printing. You use the monitor to select images for printing when you bypass the computer to print directly from the camera.

On cameras that let you compose the image on the monitor, the displayed image is taken directly from the image sensor, so it is a true TTL (through-the-lens) view. Although you can use the monitor to compose photos, there are times when you may not want to for the following reasons.

■ Battery drain. Large monitors drain batteries quickly, so it's best to keep them turned off and use the optical viewfinder for taking pictures.

■ Glare. The image on the monitor can be difficult to read in bright sunlight.

■ Steadiness. You may have to hold the camera at arm's length, an awkward position that tends to introduce blur into your images through camera shake.

Although you may want to keep the monitor turned off to conserve battery power, there are a few situations in which it becomes indispensable.

■ Close-ups. When using a camera that isn't an SLR for close-ups, the monitor is a great way to compose and focus the image since it shows the scene exactly the way it will be in the image you'll capture.

■ Odd angles. When photographing over a crowd, at ground level, or around a corner, a camera with a rotating and swiveling monitor lets you compose the image without holding the camera up to your eye.

Because an optical viewfinder is offset from the lens, what you see through the viewfinder (top) is different from the image you actually capture (bottom).

Electronic viewfinders are small flat-panel displays inside the viewfinder. Courtesy of Zight.

IOI

A common monitor icon.

In this cutaway view of a Canon SLR you can see the mirror that bounces light up into a prism for the viewfinder. The mirror swings up out of the way when you take a picture. Courtesy of Canon.

VIEWFINDERS

Viewfinders are ideal for following fast action as it unfolds—waiting for the decisive moment. One of their advantages is that they don't draw battery power so your batteries last longer. Viewfinders are coupled to the zoom lens and show the same area covered by the image sensor. There are three kinds of viewfinders and most photographers would consider the SLR viewfinder the best.

■ Optical viewfinders on SLR cameras show the scene through the lens (TTL) just as 35mm SLRs do. A mirror bounces light coming through the lens into a prism that directs it out of the viewfinder. When you take a picture, the mirror swings up to let light hit the shutter and image sensor. These are true "what you see is what you get" viewfinders because you see exactly what the lens sees.

■ Optical viewfinders on point-and-shoot cameras show the scene through a separate window that is slightly offset from the view seen by the lens. The offset view isn't a problem except in close-up photography where parallax causes you to see a view that is slightly offset from the one lens sees so a subject centered in the viewfinder won't be centered in the image.

■ Electronic viewfinders use a small LCD monitor built into the viewfinder that shows you the same through-the-lens image seen by the image sensor. Because these displays are electronic, menus can be superimposed over the scene so you can change settings without lowering the camera from your eye. This is especially useful on bright days when a monitor is hard to read because of glare. It's also advantageous for people who need reading glasses because the menu can be read without glasses.

Chapter 2
Controlling Sharpness

CONTENTS

One of the first things you notice about a photograph is whether or not it is sharp. Extremely sharp photographs reveal a richness of detail, even more than you would normally notice in the original scene. If the entire image isn't sharp, your eye is immediately drawn to the part that is. If your photos aren't as sharp as you want them to be, you can analyze them to see what went wrong.

■ **Focus**. If none of your image is sharp, or if your main subject is not sharp but other parts of the photograph are, your camera was improperly focused.

■ **Depth of Field**. If your central subject is sharp but the background or foreground is less so, you didn't have enough depth of field.

■ **Camera Movement**. If the image is blurred all over, with no part sharp, the camera moved during the exposure. Some points appear as lines, and edges are blurred.

■ **Subject Movement**. When some of the picture is sharp but a moving subject appears blurred, your shutter speed was too slow.

In this chapter you'll see how to ensure your photos are sharp when you want them to be and how to use blur creatively.

ELIMINATING CAMERA MOVEMENT

Unwanted camera movement when the shutter is open is one of the major causes of unsharp photographs. You can reduce this problem in bright light and when using flash simply by holding the camera steady and depressing the shutter button smoothly—pausing halfway down until focus locks. At slow shutter speeds, such as those you get in dim light, particularly with a long focal length lens or a lens zoomed in to enlarge a subject, you need a camera support.

The camera was steady in the left picture and moved in the right one.

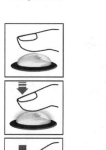
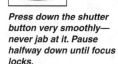

Press down the shutter button very smoothly— never jab at it. Pause halfway down until focus locks.

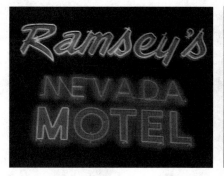

HOLDING THE CAMERA

As you zoom the lens in on a subject, you increase the focal length of the lens. As you zoom back out, you reduce it. On an SLR camera you can do the same thing by changing to a telephoto or wide-angle lens. As the focal length changes, so does the minimum shutter speed you need to hand-hold the camera without getting any blur from camera movement. The rule of thumb is never to hand-hold the camera at a shutter speed lower than your lens' focal length. For example, when using a 35mm lens you can use a shutter speed of 1/30. When using a 200mm lens, you should increase the shutter speed to at least 1/250.

When taking a photo without a support, brace the camera against your face. Just before taking a shot, inhale deeply, then exhale and hold your breath while smoothly pressing the shutter button down.

SUPPORTING THE CAMERA

When not using flash in dim light, you need to support the camera to prevent blur in your images. One way to do this is to lean against a wall or tree and brace yourself with your elbows tight to your body. You can also find a branch or railing to rest the camera on. For real stability you need a tripod, or an even easier to carry monopod.

USING THE SELF-TIMER OR REMOTE CONTROL

Almost all digital cameras have a self-timer and a few have a remote control. Although often used to give you time to get into the picture, the self-timer is also a great way to reduce blur when photographing in dim light. Just place the camera on any secure surface, compose the image, and use the timer or remote to take the picture. Don't stand in front of the camera when you press the shutter button to start the timer. If you do so, you'll prevent the camera from focusing correctly. If using the timer to photograph yourself, point it at something at the same distance you will be after scrambling into position and press the shutter button to lock focus and start the timer.

> ## HOW TO: REDUCING BLUR
> Check your camera manual for a section on the *self-timer* or *remote control:*
> _____
> _____
> _____
> _____

A self-timer icon.

When using the viewfinder for both horizontal and vertical photographs use your right finger to press the shutter button and your left hand to support the camera.

When using the monitor (left), hold the camera with both hands and brace your elbows to your sides.

If your monitor swings and tilts (right), you can steady the camera on the ground and even shoot up at flowers and other small subjects.

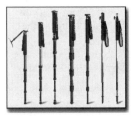

Monopods are light, collapsible, and easy to carry. Courtesy of Gitzo at (www.gitzo.com).

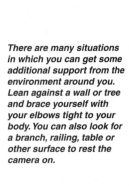

There are many situations in which you can get some additional support from the environment around you. Lean against a wall or tree and brace yourself with your elbows tight to your body. You can also look for a branch, railing, table or other surface to rest the camera on.

INCREASING SENSITIVITY

One way to improve sharpness in dim light is to increase the camera's sensitivity. This works in places such as theaters and gyms where subjects are too far away for flash to work and where you need a faster shutter speed to eliminate blur. It also is a good way to get pictures without using flash in places such as concerts and museums where flash is prohibited.

Sensitivity is usually specified as an ISO setting just as the speed of film is. Increasing the camera's sensitivity or ISO means less light is needed for a picture so you can use a faster shutter speed to freeze action or reduce blur caused by camera movement. Sensitivity on some cameras can be set between 50 and 6400, a range of 8 stops, but most offer a smaller range of settings. The price you pay for using the higher settings is noise—randomly spaced bright pixels concentrated in dark areas of the image. The more you increase sensitivity, the more noise you get. This is because digital cameras increase sensitivity by amplifying the signals captured by the photosites on the sensor—similar to turning up the volume on the radio. Dim light can be made brighter this way but unfortunately, amplifying the image also amplifies noise. Many cameras have a noise reduction mode designed to reduce or eliminate noise caused by long exposures. Some allow you to turn this mode on and off.

Noise appears in images as random color pixels especially when you use long shutter speeds or high ISO settings.

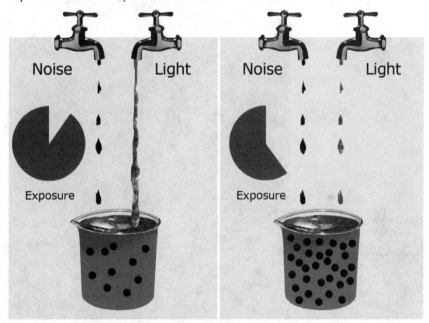

During a normal exposure the drip, drip, drip of noise is overwhelmed by the strong light from the scene. There isn't time for noise to build up in the image.

During a long exposure the noise and the light from the scene are more equal and before the image is fully exposed, noise has time to accumulate.

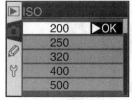

You normally change the ISO using a dial or menu.

HOW TO: INCREASING SENSITIVITY (ISO)
Look in your camera manual for a section on *sensitivity, ISO,* or *noise reduction*:

_____

_____

Sharpness Isn't Everything

Your photos don't always have to be sharp to be effective. In many cases, it's better to have part of the scene sharper than the rest. Your pictures can be sharp or unsharp in different ways. The first way concerns motion. Several factors affect the way motion is captured in images. These include your image sensor's speed, the overall brightness of the scene, lens focal length, and subject speed, direction, and distance. Another kind of sharpness concerns depth of field, how much of the scene will be sharp in the image. Even if you are photographing a static scene, part may not be sharp in the picture if you do not have enough depth of field. However, a shallow depth of field can be used to make a busy background less distracting by having it out of focus in the picture.

Motion in a scene can be frozen or blurred depending on the shutter speed and other factors. Blur can be used creatively to evoke a feeling of motion as in this shot of a waterfall in Yosemite National Park.

Shallow depth of field can focus attention on a foreground subject by making the background less sharp.

HOW TO PHOTOGRAPH MOTION SHARPLY

TIP

To capture fast action, point the camera toward where the action will occur and press the shutter button halfway down to set focus and exposure. Hold the button down until the action happens and you'll be able to get a shot off a lot faster.

The sharpness of different parts of an image helps direct the viewer who tends to look first at the most sharply focused part of the picture. In addition, sharpness itself can be part of the message of the photograph. The immobility of a frozen figure can be made more apparent by blurring people moving in other parts of the image.

Blur in a photo is caused when all or part of a subject focused onto the image sensor moves when the shutter is open. To show a moving subject sharply, the shutter needs to open and close before the image focused onto the sensor moves a significant amount. In other words, you need to use a fast shutter speed. But just how fast is fast enough? The answer depends on several factors which makes it hard to always predict how motion will be portrayed in the final photograph. To be safe, use different settings while taking more than one shot. Try shooting from a different angle or perhaps wait for a pause in the action. You are much more likely to get a good shot if you have several to choose from. Just be aware that sharpness and blur are hard to evaluate on the camera's monitor.

SPEED OF SUBJECT

The faster a subject is moving, the faster the shutter speed you need for a sharp image. However, it's not the speed of the subject in the real world that determines blur. It's how far the subject moves on the image sensor while the exposure is being made. This depends not just on the subject's actual speed, but also on the direction of its movement, its distance from the camera, and the focal length of the lens.

The shutter speed froze the central dancer but was slow enough to blur the others. This makes the central dancer the most important person in the photograph.

DIRECTION OF MOVEMENT

When the shutter is open, a subject moving parallel to the image sensor will cross more of the pixels on the sensor and be more blurred than a subject moving directly toward or away from the camera. This is why you can use a slower shutter speed to sharply photograph a subject moving toward or away from you, and not the same subject moving from one side of the scene to the other at the same speed.

DISTANCE TO SUBJECT AND FOCAL LENGTH OF LENS

If a subject is close to the camera, even slight movement is enough to cause blur. A subject—or part of one—far from the camera can move a considerable distance before its image on the image sensor moves very much. The focal length of the lens affects the apparent distance to the subject. Increasing the focal length of your lens—for example, zooming in on a subject—has the same effect as moving closer to your subject. The more you are zoomed in on it, the less a subject has to move in order to have its image move far enough on the image sensor to appear blurred. To visualize the effects of distance on blur, look out the side window of a speeding car (but not when you're driving). The objects in the foreground seem to fly by while those on the horizon don't seem to move at all.

The shutter speed needed to control the sharpness of a moving object is determined by the subject's speed, direction of movement, and distance.

On this speeding train, the part closest to the camera looks the most blurred while the farthest part looks sharper. Since all parts of the train are moving at the same speed, this shows how distance affects blur.

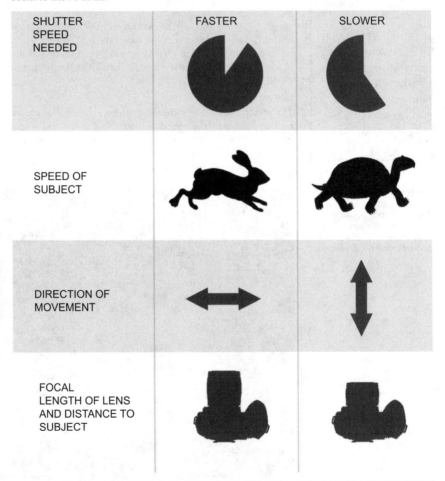

SHUTTER SPEED NEEDED	FASTER	SLOWER
SPEED OF SUBJECT		
DIRECTION OF MOVEMENT		
FOCAL LENGTH OF LENS AND DISTANCE TO SUBJECT		

HOW TO: INCREASING SHARPNESS OF MOVING OBJECTS
■ Photograph fast moving subjects heading toward or away from you.
■ Move farther back from the subject or use a shorter focal length lens.
■ Switch to shutter-priority mode and select a fast shutter speed such as 1/500.
■ Increase the ISO although this adds some noise to the image.

FOCUS

One of the first things you usually think about when taking a photo is focusing. This is an important decision because a lens can only bring one part of the scene into the sharpest possible focus. This part of the scene falls on what is called the *plane of critical focus*. Subjects falling on this plane will be the sharpest part of the picture. You move this plane toward and way from the camera as you focus.

PLANE OF CRITI-CAL FOCUS

The plane of critical focus in your image will be the area that falls on the active focus area. As you point the camera at various subjects and press the shutter button halfway down, you'll see the subjects pop into focus in the viewfinder.

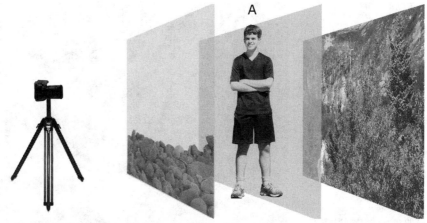

A

Imagine the part of the scene on which you focus (A) as a flat plane, much like a pane of glass, parallel to the back of the camera or the image sensor. Objects falling exactly on this imaginary plane will be in critical focus and be the sharpest part of your picture. This plane of critical focus is a very shallow band and includes only those parts of the scene located at identical distances from the camera. As you point an autofocus camera at objects nearer or farther away in the scene, the camera refocuses and the plane of critical focus moves closer to or farther from the camera. As the plane moves, objects at different distances from the camera come into or go out of critical focus.

FOCUS SETTINGS

There are three ways cameras focus—fixed focus, autofocus, and manual focus.

■ **Fixed focus** is found on the least expensive cameras, almost all camera phones, and one-time-use cameras. It is sometimes called focus-free for marketing purposes, a euphemism one reviewer suggests they change to *unfocusable*.

■ **Manual focus** found on SLRs and some expensive fixed lens cameras lets you focus by turning a ring on the lens. On point and shoot cameras you often have to use buttons or dials—a slow and awkward process at best.

■ **Autofocus** is available on all but the very cheapest cameras. In fact, on many low-end cameras it's the only kind of focus. When you press the shutter button halfway down, the camera automatically focuses on the center of the scene or some other designated focus area. A few cameras have a feature called *servo focus* that keeps a subject in focus as it moves toward or away from the camera. Autofocus often has trouble focusing on off-center subjects or on scenes with little contrast, when the object in the focus zone is brighter than the rest of the scene, when the subject is poorly illuminated, when both near and distant objects fall within the focus zone, or when the subject is moving quickly. If the camera can't focus, some cameras beep or blink a lamp. If this happens, use focus lock to focus on a subject at the same distance. Some cameras also let you switch to manual focus.

Shutter buttons have two stages. When pressed halfway down, the camera sets and locks focus (and often exposure).

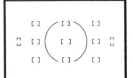

It seems the more expensive the camera, the more focusing points you get to choose from. These are from a Nikon SLR.

FOCUS ZONES

Some cameras put more than one focus zone or area, usually indicated on the screen or monitor with rectangles or brackets. Others offer a focus area you can move to position it over any point in the scene. Both approaches make it easy to focus on off-center subjects. If the camera displays multiple focus zones, it will usually focus on the center one or on the part of the scene closest to the camera covered by one of the zones. What makes zones especially useful, is that most cameras allow you to manually select the one you want to use.

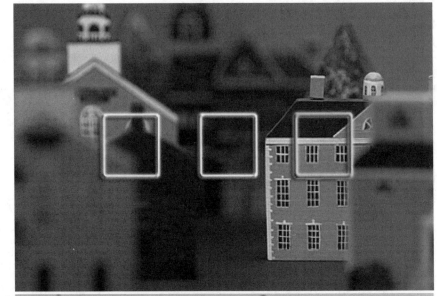

Here three areas are indicated with the active one used to set focus shown in green. The camera normally chooses the focus point that covers the closest part of the scene but you can also select the point manually.

Some cameras let you move the focus area around the screen. You may also be able to link spot metering to the focus area.

When focusing you should also be checking composition. One thing we often forget is to check how the main subject relates to the background.

Pressing the shutter button halfway down locks focus and pressing it all the way down takes the picture.

1. When photographing an off-center subject, you position the focus area, in this case the center of the viewfinder, over the subject and press the shutter button halfway down to lock focus.

2. Without releasing the shutter button, compose the image the way you want it and press the shutter button the rest of the way down to capture it. If this hadn't been done here the camera would have focused on the wall.

USING FOCUS LOCK

To change the position of the plane of critical focus, you can use a procedure called *focus lock*. Most digital cameras have a two-stage shutter button. When you press it halfway down, it sets focus and exposure and locks them in. Some cameras beep and illuminate a lamp when these readings are locked in. If you don't release the shutter button you can then recompose the image and the settings remain unchanged. This lets you focus on any part of a scene and control both focus and depth of field.

FOCUS ASSIST

Some cameras have a focus assist light that makes it easier to focus in dim light. These lights illuminate the scene, but work only at a short range.

HOW TO: CHANGING THE FOCUS METHOD
Look in your camera manual for a section on *focus-lock, manual focus,* or *focus controls*:
_____
_____

DEPTH OF FIELD

TIP

To control depth of field, switch to aperture priority mode and select a small aperture for great depth of field or a large aperture for shallow depth of field.

As you've seen, a lens can only bring objects at a single distance from the camera into sharp focus. But if you look at photographs, you can see a considerable area of the scene from near to far that appears sharp. Even though theoretically only one narrow plane is *critically sharp*, other parts of the scene in front of and behind the most sharply focused plane appear *acceptably sharp*. This area in which everything looks sharp is called *depth of field*. Objects within the depth of field become less and less sharp the farther they are from the plane of critical focus. Eventually they become so out of focus that they no longer appear sharp at all.

Often it doesn't matter so much exactly what you are focused on. What does matter is whether or not all of the objects you want to be sharp are within the depth of field so they appear sharp. If you want a large part of the scene to be sharp, you can increase the depth of field. You can decrease it if you want less of the scene sharp. In some scenes, you can significantly increase or decrease the depth of field simply by shifting the point on which you are focused or by changing the aperture setting.

A small aperture gave enough depth of field to keep both foreground and background figures sharp.

The near and far limits of depth of field are shown here as two planes (B and C), parallel to the plane of critical focus (A). Actually, they are usually not visible as exactly defined boundaries. Nor can you usually find the plane of critical focus by looking at a picture. Instead, sharp areas imperceptibly merge into unsharp ones. Notice that in the diagram the depth of field is not evenly divided. At normal shooting distances, about one-third of the depth of field is in front of the plane of critical focus (toward the camera), and two-thirds is behind it (away from the camera). When the camera is focused very close to an object, the depth of field becomes more evenly divided.

CIRCLES OF CONFUSION

Depth of field is a result of different parts of a scene coming into sharp focus at different points inside the camera.

■ Points in the scene that fall on the plane of critical focus are projected as points onto the sensor.

■ Since the light forming these points is cone shaped, any point in the scene in front of or behind the plane of critical focus is projected onto the sensor as a circle, not a point. Called *circles of confusion*, these circles increase in size the farther they are from the plane of critical focus. The point at which they expand from sharp points to out-of-focus circles defines the planes of near and far focus, between which lies the available depth of field.

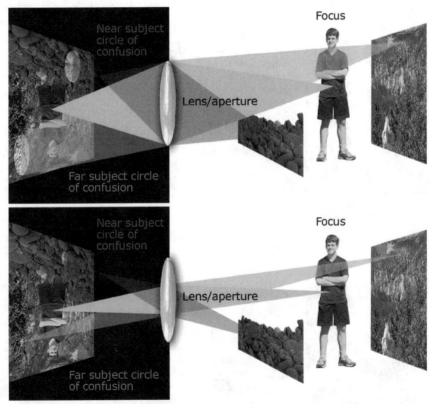

When a large aperture is used (top), the cone of light is wide and circles of confusion get larger quickly, making depth of field shallower. Smaller apertures (bottom) have narrower cones of light so the circles get larger more slowly so depth of field is greater.

CONTROLLING DEPTH OF FIELD

Here the greatest possible depth of field was used to keep everything sharp from the fighter's needle nose to the background.

Sharpness—or the lack of it—is immediately noticeable when you look at a photograph. If you are making a portrait, you want only the person to be sharply focused, but not a distracting background. In a landscape, on the other hand, often you will want everything sharp from close-up rock to far away mountain. Once you understand how to control depth of field, you will feel much more confident when you want to make sure something is—or isn't—sharp.

To control depth of field, you have three factors to work with.

■ **Aperture size**. The smaller the aperture, the greater the depth of field. The larger the aperture, the shallower the depth of field.

■ **Camera-to-subject distance**. As you move father from the subject you are focused on, you increase depth of field. As you move closer, you decrease it.

■ **Lens focal length**. Using a wide-angle lens or zooming out increases depth of field. Using a long lens or zooming in decreases it.

Each of these three factors affects depth of field by itself, but even more so in combination. You can get the shallowest depth of field with a lens zoomed in on a nearby subject using a large aperture. You get the greatest depth of field when you are far from a subject, with the lens zoomed to a wide angle, and using a small aperture.

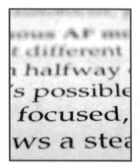

This photo of a page from a book shows how shallow depth of field can be when you get close to a subject.

Here the camera's depth of field was just deep enough to keep the bird in focus. Parts of the image closer to the camera and further away become increasingly less sharp.

EFFECT ON DEPTH OF FIELD	DEEPER	SHALLOWER
APERTURE SIZE		
CAMERA TO SUBJECT DISTANCE		
FOCAL LENGTH OF LENS		

USING MAXIMUM DEPTH OF FIELD

A wide-angle lens with a small aperture keeps everything in the foreground and background in focus.

Often you will want to get as much depth of field as possible because important parts of a scene that you want sharp are both near to and far from the camera. Maximum depth of field seems particularly important for photographs of landscapes and other scenes where a distant horizon is a part of the picture.

When a subject extends to the far distance, many photographers unthinkingly focus on that part of the scene. When you are focused on that distant point everything from that point and beyond will be sharp. But since one-third of the available depth of field falls in front of the point on which you are focused and two-thirds behind it, you are wasting two-thirds of your depth of field because everything past the focus point is going to be sharp anyway. That may mean that some other part of the scene in the foreground will not be included in the one-third remaining depth of field and consequently will not be sharp.

Instead of focusing on infinity, if you focus on some object one-third of the way between you and the horizon, you will have brought forward the point on which you are focused and so increased the depth of field in the foreground of your picture. This new point of focus is called the *hyperfocal distance*. You can use this procedure not just for landscapes, but whenever you want to shift depth of field toward and away from the camera.

When you focus on the most distant part of the scene, here it's the mountains, all available depth of field to the right of that point is wasted. As a result, the middle and foreground are not sharp because they don't fall within the range of available depth of field.

By focusing on the hyperfocal distance, the most distant part of the scene remains in focus but the near point of depth of field moves closer to the camera. The entire scene is sharp.

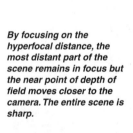

A typical infinity focus icon. A few cameras have an infinity focus mode that takes advantage of hyperfocal distance.

HOW TO: INCREASING DEPTH OF FIELD
■ Photograph in bright sun so the aperture closes down.
■ Zoom the lens out to a wider angle of view or move farther away from the subject.
■ Switch to aperture priority mode and select a small aperture such as f/11 or switch to landscape or infinity focus mode.

USING SHALLOW DEPTH OF FIELD

Shallow depth of field, sometimes called *selective focus*, is a great way to isolate a subject from a distracting foreground or background. When everything in a picture is equally sharp, the viewer gives equal attention to all parts of the scene. But if some parts of an image are sharp and others are not, the viewer is drawn to the sharpest part. You can selectively focus the camera and your viewer's attention on the most important part of the scene by limiting depth of field so the significant elements are sharp while the foreground and background are less so.

Only the bubble gum blower is sharp while figures in the foreground and background aren't.

Here attention is drawn to the sharp monarch butterfly caterpillar and the boy's face is soft and less distracting, but sharp enough that you can see the expression.

> ## TIP
>
> Digital cameras have great depth of field so you have to really push the limits to see the effects of selective focus. Move close, zoom in, and select a wide aperture.

HOW TO: DECREASING DEPTH OF FIELD
- Photograph in dim light to open up the aperture.
- Zoom the lens in or use a long lens to enlarge the subject.
- Move closer to the subject.
- Use aperture-priority mode and select a large aperture such as f/4.

CONVEYING THE FEELING OF MOTION

Panning with this barred owl blurred the background and created an impressionistic image.

Here a fast shutter speed froze everything but the ball.

HOW TO: CONVEYING MOTION

■ Try blurring images in low-light situations. In bright light, the shutter will open and close too fast.

■ Switch to shutter priority mode and select a slow shutter speed.

■ In some situations, you may want to turn the flash off when trying to blur nearby subjects.

■ Use a neutral density filter to get a slower shutter speed.

Although sharpness is a laudable goal, it isn't the only one. The creative use of blur can lead to some interesting photos—especially when conveying the feeling of motion. The shutter speed can be selected to blur some or all of an image. Many times you don't do anything but benefit from a happy accident. Anything that moves day or night is a candidate for creative blurring. Your only limitation is getting a slow enough shutter speed in bright light.

Panning the camera in the same direction as a moving subject produces an image where the subject is relatively sharp against a blurred background. Your movement should be smooth and controlled to get a good pan, so begin to pan the camera before the subject enters your viewfinder. Smoothly depress the shutter button as you follow the motion of the subject, keeping it in the same position in the viewfinder. Follow through as you would in golf or tennis. Panning takes practice so take as many images as you can. Results are quite unpredictable because your body motion adds yet another variable to the final picture.

Oops

Chapter 3
Controlling Exposure

CONTENTS

Automatic exposure control is one of the most useful features of your camera. It's great to have the camera automatically deal with the exposure while you concentrate on the image. This is especially helpful when photographing action scenes where there isn't time to evaluate the situation and then set the controls manually.

You shouldn't, however, always leave the exposure to the automatic system. At times the lighting can fool any automatic exposure system into producing an underexposed (too dark) or overexposed (too light) image. Although you can make adjustments to a poorly exposed image in a photo-editing program, you've lost image information in the shadows or highlights that can't be recovered. You will find it better in some situations to override the automatic exposure system at the time you take the picture.

Situations in which you might want to override automatic exposure often involve interesting or unusual lighting situations. For example, you need to take control when you photograph into the sun, record a colorful sunset, show the brilliance of a snow-covered landscape, or convey the dark moodiness of a forest. In this chapter you'll learn how.

THE IMPORTANCE OF EXPOSURE

Knowing how to control exposure is one of the most important aspects of photography. When a scene has both very light and very dark areas, getting the perfect exposure is a lot like parking a large car in a small garage—there isn't a great deal of room for error. The goal is to hold details in both the darkest and lightest areas so pure white is used only for spectral highlights such as reflections and pure black is used only for those few areas of the scene that are black with no details.

In this scene there are details in all of the whites that give them texture and form. The small white square has been added to give you a reference to what pure white would look like.

One of the things that makes an Ansel Adams print so stunning was his ability to hold details in both the brightest and darkest parts of a scene. To do this with film he developed the Zone System that guided him in adjusting exposure and development times for the best results. Today the adjustments are made with a photo-editing program.

In this scene there are details in the darkest shadows. The small black square has been added to give you a reference to what pure black would look like.

HOW YOUR METER WORKS

All exposure systems, including the one built into your digital camera, operate on the same general principles. A meter continuously measures the light reflecting from the subject and uses this measurement when you press the shutter button halfway down to calculate and set the shutter speed and aperture.

Your camera's meter measures light reflecting from the part of the scene shown in the viewfinder or on the monitor. The coverage of the meter (the amount of the scene that it includes in its reading) changes just as your viewfinder image changes, when you change your distance to the scene or change the focal length of the lens. Suppose you move close or zoom in and see in your viewfinder only a detail in the scene, one that is darker or lighter than other objects nearby. The suggested aperture and shutter speed settings will be different for the detail than for the overall scene.

METER AVERAGING AND MIDDLE GRAY

Your exposure meter doesn't "see" a scene the same way you see it. Its view is much like yours would be if you were looking through a piece of frosted glass.

Your meter "sees" scenes as if it were looking at them through a piece of frosted glass. It doesn't see details, just averages.

Where you see a checkerboard-like pattern (top), your camera sees only an average gray (bottom).

Every scene you photograph is something like a checker board (left), but even more complex. Portions of it are pure black, pure white, and every possible tone in between.

The exposure meter and exposure control system in an automatic camera can't think. They do exactly what they are designed to do and they are designed to do only one thing. Regardless of the scene, its subject matter, color, brightness, or composition, the meter measures only brightness, or how light or dark the scene is. The automatic exposure system then calculates and sets the aperture and the shutter speed to render this level of brightness as "middle gray" in the photograph. Most of the time this works very well because most scenes have an overall brightness that averages out to middle gray. But some scenes and situations don't average out to middle gray and that's when autoexposure will lead you astray. Let's see why.

Most scenes contain a continuous spectrum of tones, ranging from pure black at one end to pure white at the other—the *gray scale*. When shooting JPEGs there are 256 tones in the scale (2^8) and when shooting RAW images there are 65,536 (2^{16}). The tone in the middle of these ranges is *middle gray* and reflects exactly 18% of the light falling on it.

The gray scale captured in an image is a range of tones from pure black to pure white.

When you photograph a subject, your camera's autoexposure system sets the exposure so the average brightness in the image is middle gray regardless of the scene's actual brightness. As a result, when you photograph a scene with an average brightness lighter or darker than middle gray, it will be too dark or light in the image. For example, if you photograph a white card, a gray card, and a black card, and each completely fills the viewfinder when the exposure is calculated, each of the cards will be middle gray in the captured image.

Because of the way your exposure system works, if you photograph a white card, a gray card, and a black card, the exposure system sets the camera to capture each as middle gray.

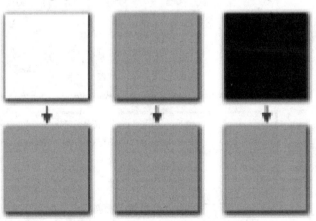

To make scenes that don't average out to middle gray appear in an image the way they appear in real life, you have to use exposure compensation or some other form of exposure control to lighten or darken the picture.

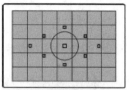

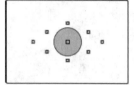

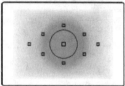

Metering patterns include matrix (top), center-weighted (middle) and spot (bottom),

When you fill the viewfinder with a gray card and press the shutter button halfway down, your camera will indicate the best exposure regardless of how light or dark the scene is.

Some cameras will recognize a backlit scene and adjust the exposure so the foreground subjects are not too dark,

TYPES OF METERING

All parts of a scene are usually not equally important when determining the best exposure to use. In a landscape, for instance, the exposure of the foreground is usually more important than the exposure of the sky. For this reason some cameras offer more than one metering method. The most common choices include the following:

■ **Matrix**, sometimes called evaluative, metering divides the image area into a grid and compares the measurements against a library of typical scenes to select the best possible exposure for the scene.

■ **Center-weighted** meters the entire scene but assigns the most importance to the center of the frame where the most important objects usually are located.

■ **Spot**, or slightly larger partial metering, evaluates only a small area in the middle of the scene. This allows you to meter just a specific part of the scene instead of relying on an average reading. This mode is ideal when photographing a subject against a bright or dark background.

Meter weighting can cause a few problems. For instance, a dark object located off center against a very light background may not be exposed properly because it is not located in the area the meter is emphasizing. Or, in some cases, holding the camera vertically may give undue emphasis to one side of the scene. These occasions are uncommon, but when they occur you can use exposure lock or exposure compensation to get a good exposure.

HOW TO: CHANGING THE METERING MODE

Look in your camera manual for a section on *metering methods* or *spot metering:*

_____

_____

_____

_____

WHEN AUTOMATIC EXPOSURE WORKS WELL

Most scenes that you photograph have an overall brightness of middle gray. Some areas of the scene may reflect 90% of the light and other parts may reflect 5%, but overall the average amount of light reflecting from the scene is 18%, the amount reflected by a middle gray subject.

Whenever you photograph a normal scene with this average brightness, your automatic exposure system exposes it correctly. Typical middle gray scenes include the following:

■ Scenes in bright sunlight where the subject is front-lit by a sun that is behind you when you face the scene.

■ Scenes on overcast days or under diffused light, such as in the shade or in evenly lit scenes indoors.

This landscape of Canyon de Chelly was taken on an overcast morning using autoexposure.

This portrait, taken under a cloudy bright sky is perfectly exposed with autoexposure.

WHEN TO OVERRIDE AUTOMATIC EXPOSURE

Not all scenes average out to middle grey. Let's take a look at some of the most common situations where your automatic exposure system will have problems and you'll need to override the suggested exposure settings.

SCENES LIGHTER THAN MIDDLE GRAY

Scenes lighter than middle gray, such as beach scenes, or bright sand or snow covered landscapes, reflect more than 18% of the light falling on them. The autoexposure system doesn't know the scene should look bright so it calculates an exposure that produces an image that is too dark. To lighten the image so it matches the original scene, you must override the camera's automatic exposure system to add exposure.

The snow scene here is typical of scenes that are lighter than middle gray. Most of the important tones in the scene are at the lighter end of the gray scale. The overall "average" tone would be about one stop brighter than middle gray. For a good picture you have to increase the exposure by one stop (+1) to lighten it. If you didn't do this, the snow in the scene would appear too gray (bottom).

SCENES DARKER THAN MIDDLE GRAY

Scenes that are darker than middle gray, such as deep shadows, dark foliage, and black cloth, reflect less than 18% of the light falling on them. Although such scenes are not as common as scenes lighter than middle gray, you will come across them occasionally. If you photograph such scenes using automatic exposure, they will appear too light. The meter cannot tell if the scene is dark or just an ordinary scene with less light falling on it. In either case it increases the exposure to make the scene lighter. When it does this, it overexposes the image and makes it too light. To produce a picture with an overall tone darker than middle gray, you need to override the autoexposure system to decrease the exposure to make it darker.

The black cat is between one and two stops darker than middle gray. To darken the scene so the cat's not middle gray, exposure must be decreased by one (-1) or two (-2) stops.

SUBJECT AGAINST VERY LIGHT BACKGROUND

Subjects against a very light background such as a portrait against a bright sky or light sand or snow, can confuse an automatic exposure system, particularly if the subject occupies a relatively small part of the scene. The brightness of the background is so predominant that the automatic exposure system reduces the exposure to render the overall brightness as a middle gray. The result is an underexposed and too-dark main subject.

Here the scenes were underexposed to silhouette the people in the foreground. To show detail in the people, exposure would have had to have been increased two stops (+2).

SUBJECT AGAINST VERY DARK BACKGROUND

When a small light subject appears against a large dark background, your autoexposure system assumes the overall tone to be darker than it actually is, because so much of the scene is dark compared to the smaller and brighter main subject. The autoexposure system increases the exposure to produce a middle gray tone. The result is an overexposed and too light main subject.

The rising sun illuminated only one boat in this harbor scene. If the exposure hadn't been reduced by two stops (-2), the background would be too light and the white boat would have been burned out and too white. A scene like this is a great place to use spot metering.

SCENES WITH HIGH CONTRAST

Many scenes, especially those with brightly lit highlights and deep shadows, have a brightness range that cannot be completely recorded by an image sensor. When confronted with such scenes, you have to decide whether the highlight or shadow area is most important, then set the exposure so that area is shown accurately in the final picture. In high contrast situations such as these, move close enough so the most important area fills the viewfinder frame. Use exposure lock from that position to lock in the exposure. Another way to deal with high contrast is to lighten the shadows by adding fill flash. A portrait, for example, lit from the back or side is often more effective and interesting than one lit from the front. But when the light on the scene is contrasty, too much of the person's face may be in overly dark shadow. In this case use fill flash or a white reflector card to fill and lighten the shadows.

> **TIP**
>
> In high contrast settings, some cameras let you decrease contrast at the time you take the picture.

The archway was in the shadows and dark while the cathedral was brightly lit by the sun. Both couldn't be exposed properly, so the archway was left as a solid black.

FOR MORE ON TEXTBOOKS IN DIGITAL PHOTOGRAPHY, VISIT HTTP://WWW.PHOTOCOURSE.COM

HARD TO METER SCENES

Occasionally it's not convenient or even possible to meter a scene. Neon street signs, spotlit circus acts, fireworks, moonlit scenes, and many similar situations are all difficult and sometimes impossible to meter. In these cases, it's easiest simply to experiment, using the exposure compensation control on your camera. After taking a picture at the suggested exposure, use exposure compensation to take other exposures both lighter and darker than the suggested settings.

This scene has a bright sky and one brightly illuminated fisherman against a dark background. A scene such as this is hard to meter because of the variety of lighting.

A relatively small subject against a wide expanse of sky will almost always be underexposed unless you use exposure compensation.

HOW OVERRIDING AUTOEXPOSURE WORKS

When a scene is lighter or darker than middle gray you need to change the exposure to capture it the way it looks or it will be too light or dark. To lighten or darken the image many cameras let you increase or decrease exposure by two stops or more. Here are some typical settings where you'd make these changes.

■ **+2** is used when the light is extremely contrasty and important shadow areas are much darker than brightly lit areas.

■ **+1** is best for sidelit or backlit scenes, beach or snow scenes, sunsets and other scenes that include a bright light source, or very light objects, such as a white china on a white tablecloth.

■ **0** (the default) is best for scenes that are evenly lit and when important shadow areas are not too much darker than brightly lit areas.

■ **-1** is for scenes where the background is much darker than the subject, such as a portrait in front of a very dark wall. Also good for very dark objects, such as black china on a black tablecloth.

■ **-2** is for scenes of unusual contrast, as when an extremely dark background occupies a very large part of the image and you want to retain detail in the brighter parts of the scene.

1. Here are three cards that you photograph with each filling the viewfinder at the time you take the picture.

2. The camera's exposure system makes all three cards appear gray in the photographs. Only the middle gray card in the center is exposed correctly.

3. Increasing the exposure for the white card and decreasing it for the black card captures them as they really appear. Only the middle gray card in the center doesn't need the exposure adjusted manually.

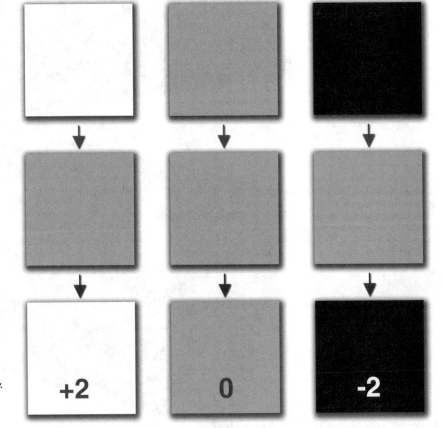

HOW TO OVERRIDE AUTOMATIC EXPOSURE

Underexposing by 2 stops kept the background dark while correctly exposing the spotlit subjects.

Most digital cameras provide ways to override the automatic exposure system to get the exposure you want. The most common choices are exposure compensation, exposure lock, or autoexposure bracketing.

EXPOSURE COMPENSATION

Exposure compensation lets you lighten or darken the photograph that the camera would produce if operated automatically. To lighten a picture, you increase the exposure; to darken one, you decrease the exposure. The amount you increase or decrease the exposure is specified in "stops." For example, to increase the exposure 1 stop, you specify +1 to open the aperture or slow down the shutter speed. It's easy to use exposure compensation because you can preview your changes on the monitor and reshoot if warranted.

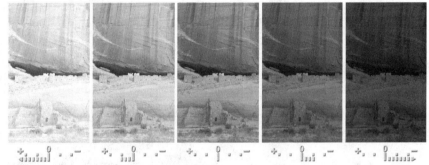

When you adjust exposure compensation you can do so in full stops and even finer increments— usually one-third (shown here) or one-half stops. On most cameras you will see a scale displayed when you use this command. The
0 indicates the exposure suggested by the camera. As you adjust the exposure toward the plus (+) side of the scale the image gets lighter. As you adjust it toward the minus (-) side it gets darker. Here you see the results as it's adjusted from +2 (left) to -2 (right). The effect of the changes on the image are dramatic.

The universally recognized icon for exposure compensation.

HOW TO: USING EXPOSURE COMPENSATION

Look in your camera manual for a section on *exposure compensation*. Many cameras let you select a setting from -2 to +2 stops in increments of 1/3 of a stop. The monitor will display the result of the changes. If you select a + value, the scene will look brighter. If you select a – value it will look darker.

_____

_____

_____

_____

_____

Pressing the shutter button halfway down locks exposure and pressing it all the way down takes the picture.

AUTOEXPOSURE LOCK (AE LOCK)

You can adjust exposures with a procedure called *autoexposure lock* (AE Lock) that works much like focus lock. You point the camera so the part of the scene you want to base the exposure on is metered (spot metering works best) and press the shutter button halfway down to calculate the exposure and focus and lock them in. While continuing to hold down the shutter button, you recompose and shoot the picture using the locked in settings. Some cameras also have an AE Lock function that lets you lock exposure independently of focus. The only real difference is that you lock exposure by pressing the AE Lock button instead of the shutter button and it remains locked until you take the picture. Focus is then determined when you take the picture, even if you have changed your position.

1. Point the camera so you are metering the area on which you want to base the exposure. Press the shutter button halfway down to lock exposure (and focus).

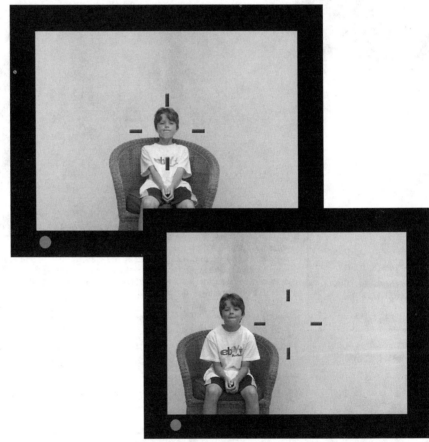

2. Without releasing the shutter button, compose the image the way you want it and press the shutter button the rest of the way down to take the photo.

If you took the picture without first locking exposure, it would be too dark because the background influenced the exposure.

A common icon for AE Lock buttons.

HOW TO: USING EXPOSURE LOCK

1. Point the camera so the subject that you want to lock exposure on is in the focus area in the center of the viewfinder.
2. Press the shutter button down halfway and hold it there to lock in the exposure.
3. Without releasing the shutter button, recompose the scene and press the shutter button the rest of the way to take the picture.

Autoexposure bracketing (AEB)

When you want to be absolutely certain you have the best exposure, autoexposure bracketing (AEB) mode takes a series of photos—each at a slightly different exposure. It's basically an automated form of exposure compensation. Some cameras let you specify both the number of exposures, usually 3 or 5 of them, and the change in exposure between each shot. Some cameras take all of the pictures with a single press of the shutter button. With others you have to press it once for each picture.

Bracketing gives you a series of images at different exposures.

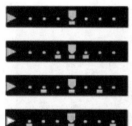

Some cameras let you select the number of shots and the exposure increment between each. Here the scale has no bracketing (top) followed by settings for one, two, and three stops difference between exposures.

The standard icon for auto exposure bracketing.

HOW TO: USING AUTOEXPOSURE BRACKETING

Look in your camera manual for a section on *autoexposure bracketing, AEB, exposure bracketing,* or *auto bracketing.*

_____

_____

_____

_____

_____

USING HISTOGRAMS

HOW TO: DIS-
PLAYING HISTO-
GRAMS
Look in your
camera manual
for a section on
histograms.

Most serious photo-editing programs let you use a histogram as a guide when editing your images. However, since most image corrections can be diagnosed by looking at a histogram, it helps to look at it while still in a position to reshoot the image. It's for this reason that many cameras let you display histograms on the monitor in playback mode or while reviewing an image you have just taken. A few cameras even let you see a histogram as you are composing an image.

EVALUATING HISTOGRAMS

As you've seen, each pixel in an image can be set to any of 256 levels of brightness from pure black (0) to pure white (255) and a histogram graphs which of those levels of brightness are in the image and how they are distributed. The horizontal axis of a histogram represents the range of brightness from 0 (shadows) on the left to 255 (highlights) on the right. Think of it as a line with 256 spaces on which to stack pixels of the same brightness. Since these are the only values that can be captured by the camera, the horizontal line also represents the image's maximum potential tonal range or contrast.

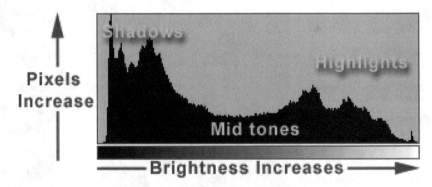

The vertical axis represents the number of pixels that have each of the 256 brightness values. The higher the line coming up from the horizontal axis, the more pixels there are at that level of brightness.

To read the histogram, you look at the distribution of pixels. Here are some things to look for.

■ Many photos look best when there are some pixels at every position because these images are using the entire tonal range.

■ In many images, pixels are grouped together and occupy only a part of the available tonal range. These images lack contrast because the difference between the brightest and darkest areas isn't as great as it could be. However, this can be fixed in your photo-editing program by using commands that spread the pixels so they cover the entire available tonal range. These controls allow you to adjust the shadow, midtone, and highlight areas independently without affecting the other areas of the image. This lets you lighten or darken selected areas of your images without loosing detail. The only pixels that can't be fixed in this way are those that have been "clipped" to pure white or black.

EVALUATING HISTOGRAMS

■ If the histogram shows most pixels toward the left (darker) side of the graph, use exposure compensation to add exposure.

■ If the histogram shows most pixels toward the right (lighter) side of the graph, use exposure compensation to reduce exposure.

The original image (top) is flat and its histogram indicates only part of the tonal range is being used. A photo-editing program was then used to expand the tonal range (bottom). You can see the change in both the image and in the histogram.

HIGHLIGHT WARNING

One thing you want to avoid is overexposing highlights so they become so bright, or "clipped", they loose details. To help you avoid this many cameras a highlight warning when you review your images. Overexposed areas of the image that have no detail blink or are outlined in color.

CLIPPED PIXELS

When a histogram shows pixels at the extreme ends of the range, in the 0 and 255 positions, it means details in those tones are lost or "clipped" in your image. These extremes should be reserved for specular highlights (reflections) and small dark shadows. When large areas lack detail an image suffers.

In the top image you can tell from the histogram that some of the highlight pixels are pure white and hence clipped. There is nothing you can do later to display details in the area of these pixels. However, if you reshoot the scene at a different exposure you can shift the pixels to the left and avoid the clipping (bottom).

To avoid clipping and better place the tonal values in subsequent shots, you use exposure compensation. Increasing exposure shifts pixels to the highlight, or right end of the histogram. Decreasing exposure shifts them the other way. Unless you are deliberately trying to get pure whites or pure blacks, you should shift the pixels if any are being clipped. This then gives you a chance to correct the image in your photo-editing program.

This series of photos was taken one stop apart using exposure compensation. As the exposure increased, pixels on the histogram shifted right. You can tell from the way the fan blades blur that the shutter speed was changed to change the exposure. In the image where it was faster, the image is darker and the blades are frozen. As slower speeds were used to increase the exposure, the images get lighter and the blades more blurred.

SAMPLE HISTOGRAMS

The way a histogram looks depends on the scene you're shooting and how you expose it. There's no such thing as a good or bad histogram. Whether a particular histogram is good or bad depends on what you are trying to accomplish. If fact, you may prefer to trust your visual reaction to the image more than the very numeric image data provided by a histogram. However, even if you never use a histogram, you can learn about digital photography by understanding what a histogram can show about an image. Following are some histograms from good images along with a brief summary of what each histogram reveals.

In this well exposed portrait there is a fairly even distribution of values in both the shadow and highlight areas of the image. There are no pure blacks in the image as shown by the gap at the far left end of the scale.

This brown moth on a gray card has most of its values in the midrange. That's why there are a number of high vertical lines grouped in the middle of the horizontal axis.

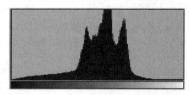

This high-key fog scene has most of its values toward the highlight end of the scale. There are no really dark values in the image. The image uses only a little more than half the camera's dynamic range.

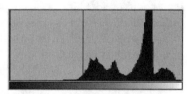

The distinct vertical line to the left of middle gray shows how many pixels there are in the uniformly gray frame border added in a photo-editing program.

This low-key scene has the majority of its values in the shadow area with another large grouping around middle gray. There are wide levels of brightness that have only a few pixels.

USING THE RAW FORMAT

One of Ansel Adam's better know expressions, drawn from his early experiences as a concert pianist, was "The negative is the score, the print is the performance." In digital photography, the image file is your score and your photo-editing program is where you perform. The printer then just does what you've told it to do as you edited the image. To get the highest possible quality, you want to start with the best possible score—a RAW image file. These files contain all of the image data captured by the camera's image sensor without it being processed or adjusted. You can interpret this data any way you want instead of having the camera do it for you. If you want total control over exposure, white balance, and other settings, this is a format you will learn to love. Only four camera settings permanently affect a RAW image. They are the aperture, shutter speed, ISO, and focus. Other settings may affect the appearance of the thumbnail or preview but their effects can be undone in an editing program. Since each camera company has defined its own proprietary RAW format, many operating systems and even photo-editing programs are unable to recognize some or all of these files. If the camera supports the RAW format the camera manufacturer always supplies a program along with the camera.

ADVANTAGES OF USING THE RAW FORMAT

There are a number of advantages to using the RAW format:

■ RAW lets you decide on most settings after you've taken the picture, not before. For example, when you shoot a JPEG image under fluorescent lights, the camera adjusts the image to remove the yellow-green tint. Any changes you make later are on top of this initial change. If you shoot the image in RAW format, the camera just captures the images as is and you decide what white balance setting to use later. You can even create different versions of an image, each with its own white balance.

■ RAW images aren't compressed using a lossy compression scheme that throws out data to make image files smaller. Although some cameras have a compressed RAW format, these images are compressed using lossless compression. When you open these images, they contain all of the original image data.

■ RAW images aren't processed in the camera as JPEG images are. When you take JPEG photos, a processing chip with the power of a small computer manipulates them based on the camera settings you have used and then compresses them to reduce their size. The changes made to your images cannot be undone later because it's the final, altered image that is saved in the image file. Some of the original image data is lost for good. With RAW images, all of the original data captured by the camera is saved in the RAW image files so you can process them later on your computer. The settings used to take RAW images are saved, but they are not permanently applied to your images until you save them in another format such as JPEG or TIFF. The images displayed on the screen when you use the camera's playback mode are just thumbnails.

■ RAW images have greater color depth and that gives you smoother gradations of tones and more colors. For example, JPEG images use only 8 bits per color (RGB) or 24 bits total. This means that JPEG images can have only 256 tones (2^8) and 16,777,216 colors (2^{24}). Meanwhile many RAW images are initially captured by the sensor in 48 or 36 bit RGB (16 or 12 bits per channel) but are reduced to 24 bit RGB (8 bits per channel) when converted into JPEG files. The full 48 or 36 bits are retained in the RAW file format after the images are processed on your computer because the original file isn't overwritten with your changes. You can even retain all 16 or 12 bits per color by saving images in a format such as TIFF and PhotoImpact's UFO format.

■ RAW images can be processed again at a later date when new and improved applications become available. Your final image isn't permanently altered by today's generation of photo-editing applications.

■ You can use a RAW image to generate alternate versions of the same image. For example, many photographers will adjust highlight and shadow areas and save these versions separately. Using a photo-editing program, they then combine the two images and by selectively erasing parts of the top image let areas of the lower image show through so all areas have a perfect exposure.

DISADVANTAGES OF USING THE RAW FORMAT

Admittedly, there are drawbacks to using RAW images—the size of their files and the need to process them. When you are done shooting for the day, there is still work to do.

■ RAW files in the camera are quite large. If you use this format a great deal you will need more storage space in the camera and computer and processing times will be longer.

■ Since RAW images aren't processed in the camera, you have to process them on the computer and this takes time. You need to convert them to another format when you want to e-mail them, post them on a Web site, print them, or import them into another program to create a slide show or publication. Many cameras help you get around this by simultaneously capturing JPEG versions at the same time they capture RAW images. You can use these more universally supported images for many of your applications and reserve the high quality RAW versions for when you need the highest possible quality.

■ RAW images are not always noticeably better. Where they shine is when you have exposure or white balance problems. Because RAW images have 16 or 12 bits per color instead of the 8 bits used by JPEG's you have dramatically more information to work with when making adjustments.

A RAW image before processing (above) and after (right).

Chapter 4
Capturing Light & Color

CONTENTS

Image sensors in digital cameras are designed to produce colors that match those in the original scene. However, there is a lot of variation among sensors and among the circuits and software that process raw images into final photographs. The results you get depend, in part, on the accuracy with which you expose the image and the match between the white balance of the sensor and the color of the light illuminating your subject.

With film cameras, photographers usually explore a wide variety of films before settling on the one or two they like best. This is because each film type has it's own unique characteristics. In some the grain is small, in others it's larger. A film may have colors that are warmer than other films, or slightly colder. These subtle variations among films are slight but noticeable and photographers gravitate to one or the other. With digital cameras, you don't have the same choice offered by film cameras. The "film" in the form of an image sensor is built into your camera. Whatever its characteristics are, they are the characteristics you have to live with until you buy another camera.

In this chapter, we explore the world of color and how you manage it in your photos.

WHERE DOES COLOR COME FROM?

Why do we see colors? Light from the sun or from a lamp seems to have no particular color of its own. It appears simply to be "white" light. However, if you pass the light through a prism, you can see that it actually contains all colors, the same effect that occurs when water droplets in the atmosphere separate light into a rainbow. A colorful object such as a leaf appears green because when white light strikes it, the leaf reflects only the green wavelengths of light and absorbs the others. A white object such as a white flower appears white because it reflects most of the wavelengths that strike it, absorbing relatively few. Inks, dyes, or pigments in color prints also selectively absorb and reflect certain wavelengths of light and so produce the effect of color.

Although light from the sun appears colorless or "white," it actually contains a range of colors similar to a rainbow. You can see these colors using a prism to separate them out.

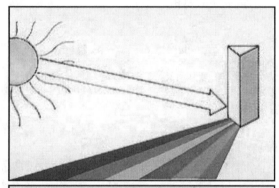

White objects reflect most of the wavelengths of light that strike them. When all of these wavelengths are combined, we see white. On the other hand, when all of them are absorbed, and none reflected, we see black.

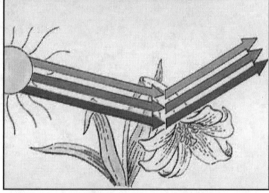

A green object such as a leaf reflects only those wavelengths that create the visual effect of green. Other colors in the light are absorbed by the leaf.

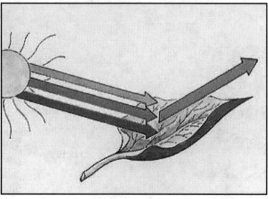

WHITE BALANCE

Although light from the sun or from a light bulb looks white to us, it actually contains a mixture of all colors, all of which affect the color of a scene it illuminates. We normally don't see the subtle differences because our brains compensate automatically. However, we do notice extremes as when the rising or setting sun casts a warm red glow over everything it illuminates. The color of the light you shoot in is specified by its color temperature in degrees Kelvin, somewhat like the room temperature is specified in degrees Centigrade. As color temperature increases, it moves through the colors red, orange, yellow, white, and blue white in that order. Daylight contains proportionately more light toward the blue end of the spectrum. Incandescent light contains more toward the red end.

Fluorescent light has a variety of color temperatures depending on its type. Some bulbs are daylight balanced.

"White" light actually contains light of different colors. The overall color cast of the light changes as the proportions of the colors change.

Color Temperature	Type of Light
12,000 K and higher	Clear skylight in open shade, snow
10,000 K	Hazy skylight in open shade
7000 K	Overcast sky
6600 K	
5900-6000 K	Electronic flash
5500 K	Midday
4100 K	
3750 K	
3600 K	
3500 K	Photolamp
3400 K	
3200 K	
3100 K	Sunset, sunrise
3000 K	
2900 K	100 watt tungsten bulb
2800 K	
1900 K	Candlelight, firelight

One way to eliminate white balance problems is to use flash since it has the same color temperature as daylight.

You can check white balance by looking at a captured image on the camera's monitor. If you examine the images closely you may notice that white areas in particular have some color cast to them. (You may want to zoom the image so you can see enlarged details more clearly.) To remove color casts and capture images with colors that look like they were shot at midday, we use the camera's *white balance* system. This system automatically or manually adjusts the image so colors are captured the way we see them regardless of the light illuminating them. For example, the fluorescent setting compensates for the greenish light from fluorescent lamps and the tungsten setting compensates for the warmer, more reddish color of tungsten lights.

Many digital cameras offer a number of white balance settings, some for specific lighting situations.

■ **Auto** (the default) works in a wide variety of lighting conditions.

■ **Daylight** is best when photographing outdoors in bright sunlight. When photographing indoors, if you like the warm glow of incandescent lights, you can capture them with this setting.

■ **Cloudy** is best when photographing outdoors in cloudy or overcast conditions.

■ **Incandescent** or **tungsten** is best when photographing indoors under incandescent lights.

■ **Fluorescent** is best when photographing indoors under fluorescent lights.

■ **Flash** is best when photographing with flash. In fact, flash is daylight balanced so it's an ideal way to remove color casts in some lighting situations.

■ **Manual** lets you set white balance manually by aiming the camera at a piece of white paper.

HOW TO: ADJUSTING WHITE BALANCE

Look in your camera manual for a section on *white balance* or *color balance*. There may be a way to set it manually for unusual lighting situations:

_____

_____

_____

_____

_____

Typical white balance icons (clockwise from top) are auto (AWB), manual, flash, fluorescent, tungsten, cloudy, shade, and daylight.

In addition to controlling white balance, some cameras also let you change the color space used to capture images from the default sRGB to the wider gamut Adobe RGB color space. sRGB, which supports fewer colors is the default color space in almost all digital cameras. Although suitable for images that will be displayed on a monitor, if you plan on editing your images and making high-quality prints, Adobe RGB is a better choice if your camera offers this option.

Color Balance and Time of Day

In photography, there is a color of light called "daylight." However, over the course of the day, the light can change from a warm red at sunrise, to a cold blue at noon, and then back to a warm red or orange at sunset. "Daylight" on the color temperature scale is really set for midday sun between 10 A.M. and 2 P.M on a clear day. During these hours, colors appear clear, bright, and accurately rendered in the photo.

Before and after midday, light from the sun is modified by the extra distance it travels through the Earth's atmosphere. Some of the blue light is filtered out, leaving the light with a more reddish cast than at midday. This is easily seen very early or late in the day when the light is often quite red-orange in tone. The change in color will affect your pictures strongly, but this reddish cast is a wonderful light to photograph in.

Just before dawn and at dusk, colors often appear muted or monochromatic. During these hours when light is relatively dim, you often have to use an extra-long exposure time.

Midday light on a sunny day produces colors that appear natural and accurately rendered.

Early morning and late afternoon light outdoors produces a warmer, more reddish color balance than you will get at midday.

For more on textbooks in digital photography, visit http://www.photocourse.com

SUNSETS AND SUNRISES

Sunsets and sunrises are relatively easy to expose because the exposure is not as critical as it is with some other scenes. If you underexpose the scene slightly, the colors will simply be a bit richer and darker. Slight overexposure will make the same scene slightly lighter.

The sun often takes on a flattened appearance as it rises above the horizon. When partially obscured and softened by a haze, its warm, red glow illuminates the foreground.

Sunrises and sunsets by themselves aren't very interesting. It's objects in the foreground, such as the skyline, or unusual atmospheric effects such as this dark cloud that give them some punch.

The colors in the sky are often richest in the half hour before the sun rises and the half hour after it sets. It pays to be patient as you watch the sky change during these periods. For one thing, the sun itself is below the horizon and not in the image so exposure problems are greatly reduced. Also, clouds in the sky often light up dramatically and in some cases, reflect the light to other clouds until you find yourself under a wonderful canopy of reflected color.

Every sunrise and sunset is unique and the variations can be truly amazing. It's certainly not true that "if you've seen one sunrise or sunset, you've seen them all." If you want the sun in the photo, it's best if it is softened and partly obscured by a mist or haze. If it rises as a hot white or yellow ball, find another subject, or turn around and photograph the scene it's illuminating.

WARNING!
Never look at the bright sun through the viewfinder. You can seriously damage you eyes.

With the bright disk of the sun included in a sunset or sunrise, your picture may come out somewhat underexposed and darker than you expected it to be. Add 1 or 2 stops of exposure to a sunset or sunrise that includes the disk of the sun.

It's tempting to take all of your photos of a rising or setting sun, but it often pays to turn around. The rich, warm light changes the colors of everything it hits. This is a magic time to capture images that will really stand out. Colors take on a warm, soft glow that can't be found at any other time of the day.

Instead of shooting into the sun at sunrise or sunset, shoot with it behind you to capture rich, warm colors of scenes bathed in the sun's light.

A long-focal-length lens will enlarge the disk of the sun so that it becomes a more important part of the picture. Foreground objects silhouetted against the bright sky, can add interest.

Here the camera was positioned so the rising sun was behind one of the grain elevators and wouldn't burn out the image with its glare.

ANTICIPATING THE SUN AND MOON

When planning to integrate the sun or moon into an image it helps to know when it rises or sets and what phase the moon is. This information is available in almanacs, and also on the Web at the U.S. Naval Observatory at http://www.usno.navy.mil.

Weather

There's no need to leave your camera home just because the sun hasn't come out. In fact, rain, snow, fog, and mist can add interest to your pictures. Objects at a distance often appear diffused and gray in such weather, with foreground objects brighter than normal because they are seen against a muted background. Remember to take a little extra care in bad weather to protect your camera against excessive exposure to dampness.

Snow covered scenes are not only beautiful to look at, they make great photographs.

A light fog or mist subdues colors and softens objects in the background.

A very light mist can dim the sun enough to include it in a photograph. If it weren't partially obscured by the fog, it would appear as a white dot against a very dark background.

Rainbows always make good pictures. The problem is, you rarely find them where you want them, when you want them. To get better at capturing them, you should know how they form so you can anticipate them. Rainbows are formed when sunlight is refracted by raindrops. You'll usually find the combination of rain and sun at the leading or trailing edge of a summer storm. You can't see rainbows at all times of the day. To understand why, visualize the way the rainbow works.

CAMERA CARE

In the cold, the monitor may be slow to come on or suddenly change color. Batteries also run down a lot faster. To prevent these problems, keep the camera under your coat so it stays warmer.

If you stand with your back to the sun while looking at a rainbow, imagine a line from the sun passing through your eye, through the Earth, and out into space. (This is called the antisolar point.) The rainbow forms a complete circle around this imaginary line, however from ground level part of it is always below the horizon. A line drawn from your eye to the top of the rainbow forms a 42-degree angle with the imaginary line from the sun through your eye. (If there is a secondary rainbow, it forms an angle of 51-degrees.) Because these angles determine the position of the rainbow in the sky, it will sink as the sun rises and rise as the sun sinks. At some points, the entire rainbow, not just the bottom half, will be below the horizon where you can't see it. That's why you'll never see a summer rainbow at midday.

Here a rainbow dramatically appears in a New England seascape.

On the coldest days of the year "sea smoke" forms over the ice-cold water. Here it surrounds a lobster boat and is backlit by the rising sun.

As a summer storm moves in, there are often times when the background is almost black with the sun shining on objects in the foreground. The contrasts can be very dramatic.

Storms are not a time to hide in the house, they are a time to get out and watch the light. As storms approach and recede, or when there are breaks in the clouds, you find some of the most interesting, at times almost surrealistic light. It's a time of muted contrasts but rich colors—a perfect environment for interesting photos.

COLOR CHOICES

The choices you make when photographing in color, such as how to position a colored object against its background or whether to concentrate on bright, brilliant colors or muted, soft ones, affect the mood and general impact of your pictures. Stop for a moment before you make an exposure and try to focus your attention only on the viewfinder image. Ask yourself how the colors relate to each other. Perhaps a change in camera position might bring one colored object to a better position in relation to another. Or perhaps you should wait until sunset turns the sky a more brilliant hue. Don't limit yourself to taking the first view of a scene that comes to your attention.

Contrasting colors can make a subject stand out, as this magenta bush stands out against the more muted green and brown background. This contrast draws the eye to the more brightly colored object in the image.

We expect certain familiar objects like human skin or green grass to be within an accepted range of normal colors. However, if the color is not known the viewer will accept a wide range of possible colors as normal.

Colors often create a psychological temperature. Blues and greens seem to be associated with coolness, water, or ice, while reds and oranges seem related to fire and warmth.

PHOTOGRAPHING AT NIGHT

You can photograph many different things outdoors at night, so don't put your camera away just because the sun is gone for the day. Light sources (street lights, automobile lights, neon signs, or fires) or brightly lit areas (illuminated buildings or areas under street lights) will dominate pictures at night because they stand out strongly against darker backgrounds. Plan to use these bright areas as the dominant part of your picture. A tripod will support your camera during long exposures and prevent blur caused by camera motion during the time the shutter is open.

Urban areas are full of bright lights that can be used to illuminate nighttime scenes.

Many cameras have night landscape and night portrait modes for taking photos at night.

Many cameras have a night portrait or night landscape mode that captures a foreground subject against a night sky or cityscape. It illuminates foreground subjects with the flash and the shutter speed is set slow enough to lighten the background. Since a slow shutter speed may be used in this mode, you need to support the camera. Also, if people are in the foreground, ask them to freeze until a few seconds after the flash has fired so the shutter has time to close, or they may be blurred. The flash is set to slow sync although you can select other flash modes.

To capture interesting images of fireworks, put people or water in the foreground. It also helps if there are identifiable objects in the image such as an illuminated building or monument to give the viewer a sense of place. Get upwind from the show since fireworks generate a lot of smoke that can become a problem if you are downwind. If you are upwind, the smoke will become part of the image, illuminated by the fireworks. Automatic exposure doesn't work well with fireworks. Try a series of exposures of different bursts because there is a certain amount of luck involved. You might also use flash or slow sync to illuminate foreground figures.

Fireworks can be dramatic, but are difficult to capture. You need to experiment and a digital camera is perfect for that because you can instantly review your results.

Set your exposure for fireworks by switching to aperture or shutter-priority mode and use a setting of f/2.8 at 1/30. You might also want to try increasing sensitivity, use exposure compensation, and try different combinations of aperture and shutter speed as well as those mentioned here.

A typical bulb icon.

Use automatic exposure at night if brightly lit areas take up most of the scene visible in your viewfinder. If they do not, use exposure compensation to reduce the exposure and darken the image so bright lights aren't overexposed.

At night you often use long exposures and some cameras have a *bulb mode*, available in the manual exposure mode, for this purpose. In this mode the shutter remains open as long as you hold down the shutter button. If it's open for more than 1 second, noise in the form of randomly-spaced, brightly-colored pixels may appear in the photograph. To reduce noise at slow shutter speeds, turn on noise reduction.

Candlelight provides a very warm glow to whatever it illuminates.

The U.S. Constitution lies floodlit in Marblehead Harbor.

This picture of Chicago was taken just after sunset through an airliner window. A few minutes later the scene was too dark to capture without blurring due to long exposure times.

There is a time at twilight and dawn where there is enough light in the sky so it has the same tonal value as the foreground.

THE MOON

The moon, especially when full, adds a lot to an image. The best time to capture the moon is when it's near the horizon. Because it is close to foreground objects at that time, it looks much larger than when it's higher in the sky.

Keep in mind that the moon is relatively dim and usually requires long exposures. Since it's moving relative to the Earth, longer exposures can actually blur it, giving it an oblong shape. To reduce the chances of this happening, shoot just before sunrise or just after sunset when there is still some light in the atmosphere from the recently set sun. (It bends around the Earth's curvature due to refraction in the atmosphere.)

The rising full moon, and the trail it leaves across the water, adds a lot to this photo of an old-fashioned coal-burning power plant on Salem Harbor.

The full moon taken with a telephoto lens on a digital camera.

Long exposures on bright moonlit nights can be very attractive. Just keep in mind that the moon does move so exposures longer than a minute or so may show it elongated.

The Direction of Light

HOW TO: PHO-
TOGRAPHING
BACKLIT SUB-
JECTS
Look in your
camera manual
for sections on *fill
flash* or *exposure
compensation*:

_____

_____

_____

The direction that light is coming from relative to your camera's position is important because it affects the shadows that will be visible in your picture. Four main types of lighting are illustrated here: side-lighting, front-lighting, backlighting, and top-lighting. Notice the position of the shadows in these photographs and how they affect the subjects.

The direction of light can also affect your automatic exposure. Backlighting, for example, can leave your subject silhouetted against a background so bright that your automatic exposure system will assume the subject is much brighter than it actually is, and so underexpose the scene and make the subject even darker. This is fine, if you want a silhouette. If you don't, you should use exposure compensation to lighten the image.

Side-lighting increases the sense of texture and volume because such cross-lighting casts shadows visible from the camera's position that emphasize surface details. Landscape photographers often prefer to work early in the morning or late in the day because the sun low in the sky will sidelight scenes and add interesting surface textures.

Front-lighting decreases visible shadows and so minimizes surface details such as skin texture. Front-lighting also tends to minimize the apparent roundness or volume of the subject.

Backlighting puts the side of the subject that is facing the camera in shade. Automatic exposure tends to make backlit scenes too dark. You can add exposure to lighten the picture, especially those parts that are in shade.

Top-lighting can occur outdoors at noon or indoors in public buildings or other places where ceiling lights predominate. If you are photographing a person, you will notice that top-lighting tends to cast shadows in eye-sockets and illuminate the top of the nose brightly. To avoid this effect, you might try moving the person into the shade.

Top-lighting, such as that found at midday, can selectively illuminate things, such as this flag in the man's back pocket, that would be in shadow with light coming from a lower angle.

THE QUALITY OF LIGHT

Light not only has direction, it can be direct or diffused. Direct light, light coming mainly from one direction, produces relatively high contrast between bright highlights and dark shadows. Diffused light bounces onto the subject from several directions, lowering contrast. Contrast, in turn, affects the brilliance of colors, the amount of visible texture and detail, and other visual characteristics.

In direct light you may have to choose whether you want highlights or shadows to be correctly rendered because image sensors can accurately record only a limited range of contrast between light and dark areas. If this creates a problem because both highlights and shadowed areas are important, you can sometimes add fill flash or reflector to lighten shadows and decrease contrast or adjust the contrast setting. In diffused light, colors tend to be softer than in direct light and textures are also softened because shadow edges are indistinct.

Direct light comes from a point source, such as the sun on a clear day. Direct light produces dark, hard-edged shadows that crisply outline details. Here the light and shadows almost form an abstraction.

Diffused light comes from a light source that is so large relative to the subject that it illuminates from several directions. On a hazy or overcast day, illumination comes from the entire dome of the sky, not from the brighter, but smaller, sun. Indoors, light bounced into an umbrella reflector or onto a wall or ceiling creates a broad source of light that wraps around the subject.

On a foggy or hazy day, objects in the foreground tend to stand out sharply against a background that is partially obscured by light reflecting from the atmosphere. You can emphasize this effect by increasing the exposure a stop or so more than recommended by your autoexposure system.

When the sky is overcast, yet still bright, interior rooms are flooded with a soft, even lighting.

USING LIGHT AND COLOR CREATIVELY

Light is one of the elements of a scene that you can alter, play with, control, and make a less or more important part of your picture. Light can make a picture ominous or airy, glowing or velvety dark. To use light creatively, you may have to override your camera's autoexposure system.

An unusual color balance can be created with an image editing program or simply by taking advantage of the existing light on a scene. Try taking one picture in the usual way, then, before you move on, see if any other alteration of the image might be feasible. There are no film costs so shoot as many pictures as you can think of. You may be surprised to discover what works and what doesn't.

Rays of light breaking through the clouds are more readily visible when positioned against a dark background, as in this scene of the sun pouring through a hole in the clouds.

When photographing sunrises or sunsets, the sun needn't be the center of interest. Here your eye is drawn to the man returning to the club from a sailing race and lifting his arms in a sign of victory.

One thing that's easy to forget is that we photograph light. In most cases, you can't create the light, you can just recognize it when it's there. It's the light that gives this image the mood it has. With most other light this scene wouldn't be anywhere near as dramatic.

Shooting into the sun before sunrise gives soft muted colors.

With backlighting, and the subject against a dark background, you can get a "halo" effect with the hair.

Sunlight filtering through an orange dome makes everything take on an orange hue.

The soft morning light on a misty day mutes the colors and gives a soft look to the image.

Chapter 5
Understanding Lenses

CONTENTS

Many digital cameras come with zoom lenses so you can zoom in or out to meet different photographic opportunities. Zoom in on a subject and you can capture a close-up portrait or distant action at sporting events. Zoom out and you can capture a wide-angle view of a large group, a roomy interior, or of an expansive landscape. The ability to change your angle of view as you frame your image is one of your most powerful creative controls. On digital SLR cameras, you can also use a zoom lens, but there are also many fixed focal length lenses available, some of them designed for specific purposes such as close-up photography.

Modern camera lenses are designed on computers, ground to critical tolerances, coated with chemicals to improve light transmission, and then mounted in precision barrels and mounts. The primary function of a lens is to gather light reflecting from a scene and focus that light as sharply as possible onto the image sensor in the camera. A high-quality lens does this very well, but to get the most out of what it has to offer you should know a few of its characteristics and how they affect your images.

In this chapter we look at lenses and their use in digital photography. This will give you the background you need to use lenses more effectively and more creatively.

INTRODUCTION TO LENSES

Point and shoot cameras often have 3x zoom lenses but they can range much higher. This camera from Canon is equipped with a 12x zoom.

Most digital cameras have a fixed zoom lens that can't be removed or replaced. One big advantage is that the camera is sealed so no dust can get on the image sensor. Digital SLR cameras have removable lenses so you can change them when circumstances dictate.

LENS INFORMATION

Many lenses display information that is useful in your photography. Be sure to take the time to read it and any printed information that came with the lens.

Focal length range as a multiplier (12x)

Focal length range in mm

Maximum aperture range as you zoom from wide angle to tele

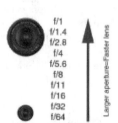

SLR cameras from major camera companies let you choose from a wide array of lenses. Here are those offered by Canon.

Information around the lens may include:

■ **The focal length** of the lens or the zoom range in mm. Here the range of a zoom lens is 6.0–72.0mm. On fixed lens cameras the zoom range is often given as a multiplier. For example, 6.0–72.0mm is 12x.

■ **The maximum aperture** or aperture range on a zoom lens. A lens' *maximum aperture* is determined by dividing the actual diameter of the aperture opening into the focal length of the lens. That's why the aperture might change from f/2.8 when zoomed in, to f/3.7 when zoomed out. Larger maximum apertures let you use faster shutter speeds to freeze action, but can add dramatically to the cost of a lens.

■ **The size of filters** or other accessories that can be screwed into the threads. The diameter is usually preceded with the symbol φ as in φ85mm.

IMAGE STABILIZATION

f/1
f/1.4
f/2.8
f/4
f/5.6
f/8
f/11
f/16
f/32
f/64

Larger aperture–Faster lens

Lenses with larger maximum apertures let you use faster shutter speeds and are often called "faster" lenses.

When you move the camera during an exposure, especially at slow shutter speeds, it causes blur in the image. To reduce this blur, some cameras have image stabilization or vibration reduction systems. These systems use a sensor to recognize camera movement and then compensate for it by shifting a lens group in the lens, or shifting the sensor in the camera. When the camera has a fixed lens, it doesn't matter which approach is used. However, on cameras with interchangeable lenses it does matter. If the system moves the sensor it will work with any lens, if it moves a lens group it only works with special lenses.

UNDERSTANDING FOCAL LENGTHS

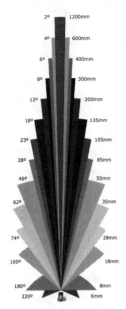

2°	1200mm
4°	600mm
6°	400mm
8°	300mm
12°	200mm
18°	135mm
23°	105mm
28°	85mm
46°	50mm
62°	35mm
74°	28mm
100°	18mm
180°	8mm
220°	6mm

The focal length of a lens determines its angle of view.

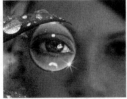

Sounds like science fiction but liquid lenses that focus by changing shape are now being used in some camera phones. Courtesy of Varioptics.

The *focal length* of a lens has a huge impact on your images and is one of the most important tools in your creative toolbox. On fixed lens cameras you change the focal length by zooming the lens. On SLRs you can also do so by changing lenses. These differences create some synonyms that can be confusing at first.

■ *Wide-angle, short focal length, short lens* and *zoom out* refer to the same thing—lenses that capture a wide expanse of a scene.

■ *Telephoto, long focal length, long lens* and *zoom in* refer to the same thing—lenses that bring distant subjects closer.

The focal length you choose is a creative choice because it has two effects on your images:

■ **Angle of view** refers to how much of a scene the lens covers. Fisheye lenses, the widest available, can capture 180-degrees. As you zoom in or change lenses to increase the focal length, the field of view narrows and you can isolate small portions of the scene without moving closer to the subject.

■ **Magnification** is related to the lens' angle of view. Since using a short focal length lens or zooming out includes a wide sweep of the scene, all of the objects in the scene are reduced to fit into the image. Zooming in or using a longer focal length lens gives a much narrower angle of view, so objects in a scene appear larger.

Lens focal lengths are based on the physical characteristics of the lens so they are absolute values. However, a given focal length lens may be a wide angle lens on one camera and a telephoto lens on another. This is because descriptions such as "wide-angle" or "telephoto" depend on the size of the film or image sensor being used. As these get smaller, a given focal length lens magnifies more. There are currently a number of differently sized image sensors used in digital cameras. For that reason, different focal lengths are needed to give the same image coverage on different cameras. Because of the confusion this causes, most digital camera companies give the actual focal length of their lenses and then an equivalent focal length were the lenses to be adapted to a 35mm camera. For example, a camera may list its lens as *7.5mm (equivalent to 50mm on a 35mm camera)*. Because digital equivalents vary widely, we often use the more familiar 35mm focal lengths in this book.

The impact of sensor size on focal length isn't limited to fixed lens cameras. Digital SLRs are often adapted from 35mm film cameras and use lenses designed to project an image circle large enough to cover a frame of 35mm film. When these lenses are used on a digital camera, the angle of view captured in the image depends on the size of the sensor placed within this image circle.

■ When the image sensor is the same size as a frame of 35mm film, called a *full-frame sensor*, then a lens' angle of view, and hence the focal length, is the same as it is on a film version of the camera.

■ When the image sensor is smaller than a frame of film, as many are, it captures a smaller area of the image circle, effectively increasing the lens' focal length by a factor of 1.5 x or so compared to the focal length indicated on the lens. Therefore, a lens that is 100mm on a film camera will be 150mm or 160mm on the digital version of the camera. This multiple works across the entire family of lenses that work with the camera, making wide-angle lens less so on a digital SLR, and making telephoto lenses more so.

A lens projects the image as a circle and the size of the film or image sensor determines what area of the circle is captured. Here the frames (from largest to smallest) show the areas captured by 35 mm film or a full-size sensor, an APS-H sensor, and a APS-C sensor.

A smaller sensor penalizes you when used with shorter focal length lenses (left). Its smaller sensor captures a smaller part of the image circle (the white outline) than a camera using a full frame sensor or film so it has a longer effective focal length

A smaller sensor gives you a bonus when used with long focal length lenses or macro lenses (right). Its smaller image sensor captures a smaller part of the image circle (the white outline), increasing magnification.

ZOOM LENSES

Most fixed lens cameras have a built-in zoom lens and zooms are also very popular with SLR users. These lenses are popular because they let you choose any focal length within the range the lens is designed for. The range is indicated in mm and on some fixed lens cameras as a multiple. For example, a camera with a range of 28–90mm is also called a 3x zoom (90 divided by 28 is about 3). A lens with a zoom range of 6–72mm would be called a 12x lens (72 divided by 6 is 12).

Zooming a lens is a little like walking toward or away from the scene. Here, a lighthouse in Maine is photographed from the same spot with the lens zoomed from wide-angle to telephoto.

If your camera has a zoom ring on the lens, you can turn it during a slow exposure to streak lights.

HOW TO: ZOOMING THE LENS
To zoom on most fixed lens cameras you press a lever in one direction or press a zoom-out button to widen the angle of view. You press the lever in the other direction, or press a zoom-in button to enlarge subjects. On SLRs and some fixed lens cameras you turn a ring on the lens

NORMAL FOCAL LENGTHS

A "normal lens" for a 35mm camera usually refers to a fixed focal length lens of 50mm or a zoom lens zoomed in a little from its widest angle. When using a lens of this focal length, the scene looks about the same as it does to the unaided eye. With a longer focal length, everything appears closer than it actually is. With a shorter focal length, everything looks farther away.

A normal-focal-length (50mm) lens isn't necessarily the one photographers normally to use. Many photographers prefer the wider angle of view and greater depth of field provided by a slightly shorter focal length.

It's hard to look at a photo and tell what focal-length lens was used to take it. However, objects in an image taken with a normal lens look normal in their spatial relationships.

SEE FOR YOURSELF

A lens is called *normal* because it captures a scene just as the human eye sees it. This seems to violate common sense because the eye's angle of view is much wider than any normal lens. However, you can demonstrate for yourself why a specific focal length is normal for your camera. While a passenger in a car, try zooming the lens or using a longer lens as you watch the traffic ahead on the monitor. The longer focal length makes distant cars appear right on top of you; in reaction you might even try to put on your brakes and then discover the cars are nowhere near as close as you thought. With shorter focal lengths, cars look far ahead, even when relatively close. A normal focal-length makes the cars appear in the same distance relationship as you perceive them ordinarily.

Another demonstration is to take two photographs of greatly different size and tape them to a wall. Look at them one at a time on the camera's monitor with the lens zoomed to a normal focal-length a little above it's widest angle. Move close enough so each fills the monitor. You'll discover you are at the correct distance for viewing the prints. With a longer focal-length you would feel too far away, and with a shorter one too close.

SHORT FOCAL LENGTHS

Using a short focal length lens or zooming out gives you a wide-angle of view that lets you capture a wide expanse of a scene. This view is ideal for use in tight spaces, such as when photographing landscapes and in small rooms where you can't position the camera a great distance from the subject.

If you don't get too close to your subjects, wide angle zoom is good for indoor portraits where including the setting is important.

A lens zoomed to a wide-angle also has great depth of field. This makes short lenses good for street or action photographs. When out to capture quickly unfolding scenes, keep the lens zoomed out to a wide angle so you'll have maximum depth of field when you respond quickly to a photo opportunity.

Zooming out increases depth of field and widens the angle of view making it ideal for interior shots. The great depth of field also makes focusing less critical so you can capture those fleeting moments you might otherwise miss.

Wide-angle lenses can distort objects near the edge of the frame. This is called "barrel distortion."

Short lenses also let you focus very close to your subject, and the effect this can have on the perspective in your images can be dramatic. Objects very close to the camera loom much larger than those farther in the background. This distortion in the apparent size of objects can deliberately give emphasis and when carried to an extreme, give an unrealistic appearance to a scene.

If your camera has a fixed lens, you may be able to use a wide-angle lens converter to widen its angle of view even more.

Wide-angle lenses have tremendous depth of field. Here one was used to shoot through a toy space station and make Quinlan look like a giant.

To improve image quality Kodak introduced a camera with two lenses, one for wide-angle coverage.

Shooting down on these two girls makes their heads look much larger than they really are since they are much closer to the camera and its wide-angle lens.

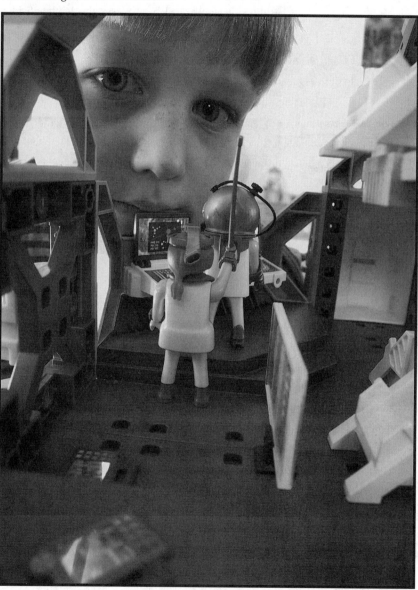

LONG FOCAL LENGTHS

A long focal length lens acts somewhat like a telescope in that it magnifies the image of your subject. This is especially useful when you can't get close to your subject—or don't want to. Long lenses are ideal for wildlife, portrait, and candid photography, whenever getting close to a subject might disturb it.

As the focal length of a lens increases, the depth of field gets shallower so you must focus more carefully. Also, a long lens visually compresses space, making objects in the scene appear closer together than they actually are. The primary drawback of a long lens is that most (but not all) such lenses have a smaller maximum aperture. This may force you to use a slower shutter speed. Since a long lens magnifies movement, just as it magnifies the subject, you may also have to use a tripod instead of hand-holding the camera. If your camera has a fixed lens, you may be able to use a tele lens converter to give it an even longer focal length.

A long lens makes distant objects appear compressed. Here a long lens has been used to "compress" a street scene at the foot of the Rocky Mountains in Colorado.

A long lens doesn't compress space (bottom), it just captures the compression that's already in the distant part of a scene (top).

When the lineup of cement trucks (bottom right) is shot head-on with a long lens (above left) they appear much closer together then they really are. This is actually due to the distance from the subject, not the focal length of the lens, but the effect is easy to get with a long lens.

A long lens makes the sun look larger in relation to foreground objects.

A long lens is essential for much nature photography.

These two photos were taken with the same camera. One was taken using optical zoom (top) and the other with digital zoom from farther away (bottom). The one taken with optical zoom is much sharper.

DIGITAL ZOOM

Zoom comes in two varieties; optical and digital. An *optical zoom* actually changes the amount of the scene falling on the image sensor. Every pixel in the image contains unique data so the final photo is sharp and clear. A *digital zoom,* found on many fixed lens cameras, uses sleight of hand by taking a part of the normal image falling on the sensor and then enlarging it to fill the sensor. It does this by adding new pixels to the image using interpolation. The interpolated image doesn't have as many unique pixels as one taken with an optical zoom so is inferior. In fact, you don't even need this zoom feature because you can get exactly the same effect just by cropping a normal image in a photo-editing program and then enlarging it.

HOW TO: USING DIGITAL ZOOM
Look in your camera manual for a section on *digital zoom*:

_____

_____

_____

_____

PORTRAITS AND FOCAL LENGTH

A long focal length is ideal for portraits, especially for head-and-shoulders portraits. The focal length lets you keep your distance and still fill the viewfinder frame with the subject. Keeping at a distance eliminates the exaggerated perspective caused by working very close to a subject with a shorter focal length lens. It also helps relax your subjects if they get uneasy, as many people do, when a camera comes close.

A long lens lets you get portraits without crowding in on the subject. This lets you capture more natural expressions.

Using a short focal length lens close to the subject adds some distortion to the portrait but it still works as an image. Perhaps not as flattering as it might be, the image is probably more interesting to others than to the subject.

MACRO MODE AND MACRO LENSES

TIP: CLOSE UP

For maximum magnification, follow these four steps:

1. Use macro mode or a macro lens.

2. Zoom the lens to it's longest focal length.

3. Set focus to the minimum focus distance.

4. Look through the viewfinder or use the monitor as you focus the subject by moving the camera toward and away from the subject.

In close-up or tabletop photography, digital cameras have a huge advantage over traditional film cameras because you can review your results and make adjustments as you shoot. If a photo doesn't turn out as you'd hoped, just delete it and try something new. Film photographers have to wait to get the film back from the lab before they can make adjustments. By then, the moment has passed, they have probably left the scene, taken apart the setup, or they have forgotten what it was they did. Take advantage of your instant feedback to experiment and learn.

When photographing small objects, your lens' focal length and minimum focusing distance affect how small objects are captured in photos. For example, if you're photographing a small coin, you probably don't want it to appear as a tiny coin surrounded by a large background. More likely you'd like a photo showing a large coin surrounded by a small background. For many pictures, just zooming your lens in on the subject will suffice. However, macro lenses or lenses with a macro mode allow you to get a lot closer to the subject, making it much larger in the final image. If you can't get close enough to an object to fill the image area, you can always crop out the unwanted areas later. However, the more you crop, the smaller the image becomes.

■ Point-and-shoot or other fixed lens cameras usually have a macro mode that lets you get close to a subject. When using one of these cameras, you should compose the image on the monitor, especially when closer than about 3 feet (90cm). If you don't, a subject centered in the scene won't be centered in the photo unless the camera has an electronic viewfinder so you view the scene through the lens.

■ SLRs show the scene through the lens and have macro lenses and other lenses with a macro mode that let you get closer than normal.

If you look at some close-up photographs, you will notice that very few of them appear to be completely sharp from foreground to background because the depth of field in a close-up tends to be shallow. You can increase depth of field by using a small aperture but when you get the camera really close, don't expect much depth of field—maybe less than a half-inch. It's best to arrange the objects so they all fall on the same plane. That way, if one's in focus, they all will be. Another thing to try is a shorter lens with a wider angle of view. This will give you more depth of field and include more of the background for context.

When you focus close up, keep in mind that depth of field includes the plane you focus on plus an area in front of and behind that plane. You'll find that in close-ups half of the sharpest area will fall in front of the plane on which you focus and half behind it.

HOW TO: TAKING CLOSE-UPS

Look in your camera manual for a section on *macro* or *close-up mode*:

_____

_____

_____

_____

The universally accepted icon for macro mode.

Macro lenses let you get very close to subjects but have very shallow depth of field. Here I focused on the eye of the newt so it was the sharpest part of the photo.

The ring flash fires a circle of light although the two sides can be fired independently or with different intensities.

TIP: USE THE MONITOR

When taking close-ups on a point and shoot camera without an electronic viewfinder use the monitor to compose the image. On theses cameras the viewfinder is offset from the lens so the area seen in the viewfinder will differ from the area included in the image.

Shallow depth of field has its own benefits, so you don't necessarily have to think of it as a problem. An out-of-focus background can help isolate a small subject, making it stand out sharply.

Many close-up photographs are of small objects that don't entirely fill the viewfinder frame. Automatic exposure systems can be fooled if the brightness of the small object is different from the brightness of the larger background. The meter averages all of the light reflecting from the scene and may select an exposure that makes the main subject too light or too dark. In these cases, use spot metering or exposure compensation to adjust for the background. If an image is too dark, increase the exposure. If the image is too light, decrease the exposure.

HOW TO: INCREASING DEPTH OF FIELD IN CLOSE-UPS
■ Increase the illumination of the subject to stop down the aperture.
■ Don't get any closer to the subject than you have to.
■ Focus on something in the middle of the scene (front to back) since in close-ups, depth of field is half in front and half behind the plane of critical focus.
■ To increase depth of field, switch to aperture-priority mode and select a small aperture such as f/11.

PERSPECTIVE IN A PHOTOGRAPH

A photograph can appear to compress space so that objects appear closer together than you expect. Another photograph of the same scene can seem to expand space so that objects appear farther apart than normal. These apparent distortions in perspective—the appearance of depth in a photograph—are often attributed to the focal length of the lens being used but are actually caused by your distance from the subject.

Changing camera-to-subject distance does change perspective as shown here. As the camera is moved closer to the foreground subject (bottom), the subject appears to increase in size relative to the background. This changing relationship between the size of objects in the foreground and background creates the difference in perspective.

As you move closer and select a focal length that keeps the subject the same size, the angle of view widens and the background diminishes in size.

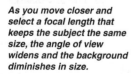

LENS ACCESSORIES

A wide-angle lens converter attached to the camera using a lens adapter.

Many lenses have threads into which you can screw filters and other accessories. Here are just some of the accessories you can attach.

■ Only a few digital cameras have interchangeable lenses. Most have a built-in zoom lens that cannot be removed. To change its focal length, you use lens converters that screw in or slide onto the zoom lens.

■ Lens hoods protect the front element from bumps and keep stray light from striking the front of the lens and causing flare or ghost images.

■ Caps protect the front and rear of the lens when it's not in use. A body cap protects the camera when no lens is attached.

■ Protect filters keep the front element of your lens from getting scratched or dirty.

■ Circular polarizing filters remove reflections from glass, water, and other reflective surfaces, darken blue skies, and improve color saturation. If you use a linear polarizing filter, you can't use autofocus.

■ Skylight filters reduce the blue casts you often get when photographing subjects in the shade on sunny days.

■ UV filters absorb ultraviolet light and cut the haze when photographing landscapes or from airplanes.

■ Neutral density filters cut the light entering the camera so you can use slower shutter speeds or wider apertures in bright light.

■ Soft focus filters soften the focus to make portraits more flattering and to make hazy, romantic landscapes.

■ Close-up lenses magnify the subject without affecting aperture settings.

■ Color conversion filters let you fine-tune the way you capture colors.

A polarizing filter (left) darkens the sky and removes reflections from foliage so it has more color. A shot without a filter is shown at the right.

Chapter 6
Using Flash & Studio Lighting

CONTENTS

Automatic electronic flash is so convenient and easy to use that you are usually unaware it even fires. With your camera on automatic, it's always ready when your autoexposure system decides it's needed. But this on-camera flash lighting has certain characteristics that can make a difference in the way your pictures look. For example, the pictures will have a "flat" lighting typical of flash-on-camera shooting. Alternative approaches, such as using an external flash to bounce light off walls or ceilings, or even just turning the flash off may produce more interesting results. In any event, you will be able to use flash to better advantage as you become more familiar with its characteristics.

But flash isn't your only source of controlled lighting. You can also use the camera in a home studio setting, perhaps taking formal portraits, or photographing smaller items for your records, insurance, sharing, or even selling on eBay.

In this chapter we explore all of these forms of lighting, from the built-in flash, to an external flash, to studio lighting. In the process you'll learn what makes lighting more effective and when, where, and how to use and control it.

HOW AUTOMATIC FLASH WORKS

Every flash has a maximum useful range. The intensity of the flash when it reaches a subject depends on the flash's power and on how far the light has to travel. The further the subject is from the flash, the less light will reach it and so the less light will be reflected from the subject back toward the camera.

The light from a flash falls off with distance. When you double the distance, you get one-quarter as much light. This relationship is called the inverse square law.

When the flash fires, the beam of light expands as it moves father from the camera so its intensity falls off with distance. As a result, subjects nearer the flash will be illuminated with a more intense light than subjects farther away. The rate at which the light falls off is described by the *inverse square law*. The law states that if the distance between the flash and subject is doubled, only one quarter the amount of light will reach the subject because the same amount of light is spread over a larger area. Conversely, when the distance is halved, four times as much light falls on a given area.

When subjects in an image are located at different distances from the camera, the exposure will only be correct for those at one distance—normally those closest to the camera or in the area metered by the autoexposure system. Subjects located farther from the flash will be increasingly darker the farther they are from the flash.

Since flash falls off with distance, objects near the flash will be lighter in a picture than objects farther away. You can use this to advantage; for example, at night you can isolate a subject against a dark background.

HOW TO: USING AUTO FLASH
Auto mode is usually the default settings. Look in your camera for a section on *auto flash*:

_____

_____

_____

_____

_____

FLASH SYNC AND SHUTTER SPEEDS

Leaf shutters, common on point and shoot cameras, allow faster flash sync speeds because they don't use curtains.

When you take a picture, the shutter opens and closes to let light strike the image sensor. When it does so, the shutter is fully open for a very short time. If the shutter speed is too fast, the burst of light from the flash won't fully expose all parts of the image sensor and part of the scene won't be captured in the image. The fastest shutter speed that can be used is called the *flash synchronization speed* and is usually between 1/125–1/500 second. If you select a faster shutter speed directly or indirectly, most cameras will override you and lower it. The shutter works with two curtains, a front and rear (sometimes called first and second curtains). The shutter opens when the front curtain slides out of the way and ends when the rear curtain slides to close it. The flash fires either when the shutter first fully opens or just before it's about to close.

■ **Front/first curtain sync** (the usual mode) means the flash fires when the shutter's front curtain first fully opens to expose the image sensor.

■ **Rear/second curtain sync** means the flash fires just before the shutter's rear curtain starts to close to end the exposure.

A focal plane shutter opens a curtain to begin an exposure and closes a second curtain to end it. At fast shutter speeds (top) the second curtain starts to end the exposure before the first curtain has fully opened so the two curtains form a slit traveling across the image sensor. Flash would only expose the area uncovered by the slit between the two rapidly moving curtains. At the flash sync speed and slower (bottom) the second curtain doesn't start to close until the first one is fully open.

Front curtain sync fires the flash at the beginning of the exposure, then records ambient light. As a result, light streaks from the moving subject appear in front of it.

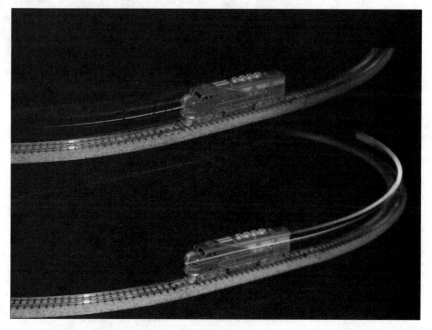

Rear curtain sync fires the flash at the end of the exposure, after the ambient light has been recorded so the streaks trail behind the subject.

Portraits with Flash

Flash is a good source of light for portraits, particularly of children. The light from the flash is so fast that you never have to worry about your subject moving during the exposure and blurring the picture. For the same reason you don't have to be quite as careful about camera motion blurring the image; you can hand-hold the camera and shoot as rapidly as the flash will recharge.

Positioning the flash and subjects
You may want to choose carefully the position of the flash. Light from a flash built-into the camera often produces less attractive results than if you use an external flash to bounce the light onto the subject off a wall, ceiling, or umbrella reflector.

When photographing more than one subject, each is given the same importance when lined up parallel to the camera because each receives the same amount of flash illumination. If they are at different distances from the flash, they will be illuminated differently. This is a good way to make one more visually dominant than others in the image.

When a subject is placed close to a wall, there will be a distracting shadow in the image cast by the light from the flash. By moving the subject away from a wall, these shadows disappear.

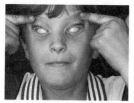

Eric shows one way to avoid red-eye.

Red-eye can look eerie and be corrected in a photo-editing program, but it's best to avoid it.

People aren't the only ones to show red-eye as shown in this flash photo of an owl.

TIP

Red-eye reduction flash works best when the subject isn't too far away and looks directly into the camera.

The almost universally accepted icon for red-eye reduction mode.

RED-EYE

When photographing people, you'll often see images with what's called "red eye." The light from a flash has entered through the subject's pupil and reflected off the back of the eye (the retina) and back out to the camera. Since the retina is lined with blood vessels, the reflected light takes on a red color. To eliminate red-eye, many cameras have a "red-eye reduction" mode. This mode works by firing a short pre-flash lamp or a burst of flashes to close the subject's iris a moment before the actual flash fires to take the picture.

To minimize red eye, you can also move an external flash farther away from the axis of the camera lens, tell the subject not to look directly at the camera, or increase the overall room lighting. You can also remove red-eye later using a photo-editing program, but it's easier to avoid it to begin with.

HOW TO: COMBATING RED-EYE
Look in your camera manual for a section on *red-eye* or *red-eye reduction*:

_____

_____

_____

_____

USING FILL FLASH

When photographing people or other subjects with the light to the side, shadow areas can be so dark in the image that they show little or no detail. When the subject is back-lit or against a bright background, it can be underexposed. To fix these problems you use fill flash—often called Flash On or Forced Flash. When using this setting, the flash fires even if there is enough available light to take the picture without flash. Fill flash is also a good way to get accurate color balance under unusual lighting.

With no fill flash (left) the bright background has caused the main subject to be underexposed. Using fill flash (right), the subject is properly exposed. Photo courtesy of Tim Connor.

Fill flash illuminates this backlit sunflower against the sky. If flash hadn't been used, the flower would have had dark shadow areas.

One reason to use fill flash outdoors is to add catch lights to eyes—hot spots that make the eyes sparkle.

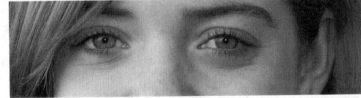

HOW TO: USING FILL FLASH
Look in your camera manual for a section on *fill flash, forced on, flash on,* or *any time flash*:

_____

_____

_____

_____

_____

The almost universally accepted fill flash icon.

FOR MORE ON TEXTBOOKS IN DIGITAL PHOTOGRAPHY, VISIT HTTP://WWW.PHOTOCOURSE.COM

CONTROLLING FLASH EXPOSURES

When using the flash, you can avoid burned out foreground subjects and other exposure problems by adjusting the flash's output, or using flash exposure lock.

Flash exposure compensation lets you manually adjust the amount of flash illuminating the subject without changing the camera's aperture or shutter speed. This is an ideal way to balance flash and natural light when using fill flash and to correctly expose scenes or subjects that are darker or lighter than normal (middle-gray). Flash exposure compensation can be set to a minus setting to make the main subject darker or to a plus setting to make it brighter. A setting on some cameras that automates this procedure is flash bracketing that takes a series of pictures at different flash intensities.

Here five photos have been taken with flash. From left to right, flash exposure compensation reduced the flash exposure one stop from one image to the next.

You can use flash exposure compensation in conjunction with regular exposure compensation. Doing so lets you use regular exposure compensation to lighten or darken the background that's illuminated by ambient light, and use flash exposure compensation to lighten or darken the subject illuminated by the flash. This is a powerful combination of exposure controls that let's you capture images just the way you want them.

Flash usually gives you very good exposures but if you block a sensor, you can get odd results like this gross overexposure.

A typical flash compensation icon.

In both images flash was used to photograph the Cardinal flower. In the image on the far right, exposure compensation was set to -2 to darken the background.

A few cameras have flash exposure lock that works much like AE lock and is used to properly expose off-center subjects. To use it, you center the main subject and press the shutter button halfway down. The flash fires a preflash to determine the best exposure and then locks it so you can recompose the image before pressing the shutter button the rest of the way down to take the picture.

USING SLOW SYNC FLASH

Icons for night portrait (left) and night landscape (right).

Slow synchro flash created this image that's both sharp and blurred at the same time.

Pictures taken with flash often show a well exposed foreground subject against a black background. Using *slow sync* flash minimizes this problem by using flash to illuminate the foreground subject and then leaving the shutter open longer than usual to lighten the background. Many cameras have a night portrait or a night landscape mode that uses this effect. On other cameras you use it by selecting shutter-priority mode and then selecting a slow shutter speed such as 1/20, but experiment because the results are hard to predict.

In many cases, the slow shutter speed used in this mode allows blur from rapidly moving objects or camera shake to appear as blur in the images. To avoid blur, use a tripod and photograph static subjects. Or, use this effect creatively. A short flash burst combined with a long shutter speed gives interesting effects. The flash freezes objects sharply, and then in the dim light, camera or subject movements blur the image to create streaks.

When using slow sync flash, some cameras let you take advantage of front or rear curtain sync (also called first and second curtain sync). As discussed on page 101 your choice determines whether the flash fires just after the front curtain opens or just before the last curtain closes. The differences can be striking. For example, when photographing a moving car at night, front curtain sync will cause the taillights to have a forward streak and rear curtain sync will cause them to have a receding streak.

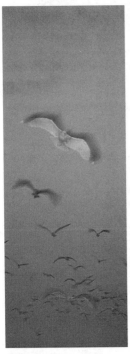

Slow sync flash outdoors at sunset captured gulls in mid flight with interesting effects.

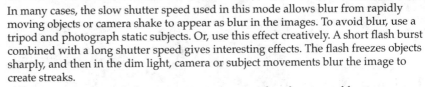

HOW TO: USING SLOW SYNC FLASH

Look in your camera manual for a section on *slow sync, night portrait, night landscape, first and second curtain sync, front and rear curtain sync*:

_____

_____

USING AVAILABLE LIGHT

The almost universally accepted flash off icon.

Here the flash was turned off in a museum and a photo was taken using just the natural light streaming in the windows.

Turning the flash off for indoor portraits can give you much more natural lighting.

FLASH OFF

When the flash is off, long exposure times may create blur in the image. At times like this, you may want to use a camera support.

There are times when the light is dim but you want to capture the unique colors of the available light. For example, you might want to capture the romantic glow of an interior space or retain the moody darkness of a shot at night. There are other situations where flash photography is not allowed. In these circumstances you need to turn the flash off or close it and support the camera for a long exposure. If you don't turn off the flash it will fire and the foreground subjects will appear as if photographed in daylight. If you don't support the camera you will likely have blur from camera movement.

HOW TO: TURNING OFF THE FLASH

Look in your camera manual for a section on *forced off* or *off* flash:

_____

_____

_____

_____

_____

When photographing in dim light there are things you can do to get better results when not using flash. Try the following:

- ■ Increase the camera's sensitivity (ISO).
- ■ Use the camera's self-timer or remote control.
- ■ Support the camera or use a tripod.

USING AN EXTERNAL FLASH

Some cameras have a hot shoe into which you can slip a dedicated flash unit.

Flash photography has come a long way since the 19th century when a photographer had to ignite a tray filled with flash powder to illuminate a scene. Almost every digital camera comes with a small built-in automatic flash that is tied into the autoexposure system. This flash is convenient, however its range is very short and so close to the lens that photos of people often capture them with red eyes. It also emits a hard, direct light and can't be rotated to bounce flash off a wall or ceiling to soften it.

For better flash photography you need an external flash that slips into a hot shoe on top of the camera, or connects to the camera with a bracket and flash cord that plugs into a flash sync terminal on the camera. (There are also slave units that have a sensor so they fire when the built-in flash fires.) If the flash is designed specifically for your camera it's called a "dedicated" flash unit, and the camera controls both the internal and external flash. Flash units not designed to work with the camera usually fire at full-strength unless they have their own output control.

One of the biggest advantages of an external flash is that you can swivel and rotate the flash head to bounce light off walls and ceilings.

Bounce flash can evenly illuminate a scene that has depth because it spreads the light more evenly front to back.

When using an external flash you can use it alone or combine it with the built-in flash for even more lighting possibilities.

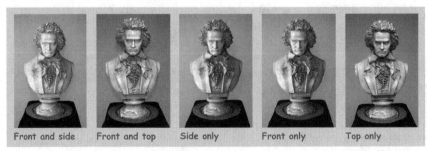

Front and side   Front and top   Side only   Front only   Top only

Some cameras let you use the built-in flash and an external flash at the same time. Here these two flash units were used to take a "portrait". The flash from the front was created by the built-in flash. That from the side or top was created when the head of the external flash was rotated or swiveled to bounce flash off the wall or ceiling.

USING FLASH CREATIVELY

Your choices with flash may be to freeze action, make its illumination obvious and noticeable in the image, or to unobtrusively raise the level of illumination in a scene that would otherwise be too dark for easy shooting.

Use flash to freeze actions that would otherwise be blurred.

By getting down at the same level, the flash portrait becomes much more interesting than if I'd stood and shot down.

By holding the flash off to the side it casts hard shadows on the wall that dramatically emphasize the subject. Courtesy of Tim Connor.

A flash captured this white moth on a pink lady slipper with great depth of field and life-like colors.

Using flash out of doors isolated the girl with the snake, making her the center of attention.

STUDIO LIGHTING

There are two important reasons to use artificial lighting in studio photography. First, increasing the level of light lets you use smaller apertures for greater depth of field, and shorter shutter speeds to reduce blur from camera or subject movement. Second, you can better control the illumination of the subject, placing highlights and shadows to reduce or emphasize modeling.

CANDIDATES FOR STUDIO LIGHTING

There are a number of subjects that lend themselves to being photographed under controlled lighting. Here are just some of them.

■ **Portraits** can be either candid or more formal. Candid portraits are usually captured during the flow of action. It's the more formal ones that give you the time needed to arrange lighting.

■ **Small objects** need to be illuminated properly to bring out details and colors. You can light a subject in several ways, depending on your objectives. For example, an object with low relief, such as a coin needs to be cross-lit to bring out details. Many objects photograph better in the diffuse lighting provided by a light tent. Flash can freeze action and increase depth of field. Your options are varied, limited only by your willingness to experiment.

When lighting flat objects you want the light even over the entire surface. To do this you set two lights at 45 degree angles so there are no hot spots or reflections. Lights courtesy of tabletop studios—
http://www.ezcube.com

■ **Flat copy** such as posters, stamps, prints, or pages from books require soft, even light over their surface and the camera's image sensor must be exactly parallel to the subject to prevent "keystoning." Even then, many lenses will curve otherwise straight lines at the periphery of the image because they are not designed for copying and introduce what's called curvilinear or barrel distortion. There are other lens aberrations that make it difficult to keep the entire image in focus at the same time. One suggestion is to use a small aperture that increases depth of field and uses the center portion of the lens where aberrations are least likely to affect the image.

LIGHTING

For good portraits or product shots, you need to improve on the camera's built-in flash. Direct on-camera flash doesn't give a picture the feeling of texture and depth that you can get from side-lighting or softer light. If you use an external flash, you can position the flash to illuminate the subject from an angle for a better *lighting effect.*

Light tent with red goblet—
http://www.ezcube.com

■ **Light tents** bathe a subject in soft, even lighting and are particularly useful for complex subjects such as bouquets, highly reflective subjects such as jewelry, and translucent subjects such as glassware. A subject placed in the light tent is surrounded by a translucent material which is lit from the outside. If the subject is small enough, you can use a plastic gallon milk bottle with the bottom cut out and the top enlarged for the camera lens. When positioned over the subject and illuminated by a pair of floodlights, the light inside the bottle is diffused by the translucent sides of the bottle. The result is a very even lighting of the subject.

■ **Studio lights** are usually just reflectors mounted on adjustable stands. Keep in mind that the color of the light you use to illuminate an object may affect the colors in the final image. For best results you need bulbs that are daylight balanced. The best of these are fluorescent because they don't give off any heat.

5000k compact fluorescent bulb highly recommended for product photography—
http://www.ezcube.com.

A light tent can make an amazing difference in tabletop photos—http://www.ezcube.com

This very complex subject was shot in a light tent. The soft diffuse light reached every part allowing it to be captured without dark shadows and burned out highlights—http://www.ezcube.com.

A medallion placed on a light box and shot from above has a pure white background. A small lamp is used to sidelight the coin to bring out its relief. http://www.ezcube.com

■ **Reflectors**. When the light illuminating a small subject casts hard, dark shadows, you can lighten them by arranging reflectors around the subject to bounce part of the light back onto the shadowed areas. You can use almost any relatively large, flat reflective object, including cardboard, cloth, or aluminum foil (crumpling the foil to wrinkle it, then opening it out again works best). Position the reflector so that it points toward the shadowed side of the subject. As you adjust the angle of the reflector, you will be able to observe its effects on the shadows. Use a neutral-toned reflector so the color of the reflector doesn't add a color cast to the image.

■ **Light panels** are an ideal source of light. When you place an object on the illuminated panel and shoot from above, the area surrounding the object is captured as pure white. If you cut a hole in a sheet of background paper and arrange it as a sweep, a glass placed on the hole appears to glow from within as light streams through the hole and through the glass. Finally, by tipping a panel on its side, it can be used as a background or used like any other light source.

■ **Flash**. There is definitely a role for on-camera flash in studio photography. It doesn't hurt to see what results you get from the built-in flash. A special kind of flash is the ring flash. These units fit around the lens and fire a circle of light on the subject. They are ideal for shadowless close-up photography such as that used in medical, dental, and nature photography. Because ring flash is so flat (shadowless), most units allow you to fire just one side or adjust the output of each side independently so the flash casts shadows that show surface modeling in the subject.

Here a crystal glass was shot in a light cube against a black background to set it off.

A hole was cut in a piece of black paper and placed on a light table. The glass was then placed over the hole and looks like it's illuminated from within.

With a white background (top) the clock is underexposed but it's not with a gray background (bottom).

BACKGROUNDS

Some thought should be given to the background you use. It should be one that makes your subject jump out, and not overwhelm it. The safest background to use is a sheet of neutral gray poster board that can be formed into a sweep, a curved "L" shape that gives a nice smooth gradation of light behind the subject. It's safe, because it reduces potential exposure problems and most things show well against it. Other options include black or white backgrounds but they may cause some exposure problems unless you use exposure compensation. Finally, there are colored backgrounds, but these should be selected to support and not clash with the colors in the subject. The texture of the background is also a consideration. For example, black velvet has no reflections at all while black poster board might show them.

There are times when you don't want a background in a photo. This silhouettes the subject against a pure white background. You'll often see this technique used in catalog photos but it's also a great way to make it easy to select an object in a photo-editing program so you can cut it out and paste it into another image. To get this effect you need to overexpose the background. In some cases this is as easy as pointing lights at it. In the case of small objects, a light panel makes it very easy.

FOCUS AND EXPOSURE

The exposure procedure for close-up and tabletop photography isn't a lot different from normal photography but you have the opportunity to control lighting. The biggest difficulty may arise from automatic exposure. Many close-up photographs are of small objects that don't entirely fill the viewfinder frame. Automatic exposure systems can be fooled if the brightness of the small object is different from the brightness of the larger background. The meter averages all of the light reflecting from the scene and may select an exposure that makes the main subject too light or too dark. To correct this, you can use exposure compensation to lighten or darken the main subject.

Macro lenses are useful when you want to get close to small subjects so they fill the frame. Just keep in mind that in close-ups, depth of field gets very shallow.

TIPS AND TRICKS

■ When taking close-ups you can use spot metering to meter just a small part of the image so the background doesn't influence the exposure.

■ When using flash for close-up images the flash may not fully illuminate the subject or be blocked by the lens. Be sure to take a test shot.

■ To control exposure, use a neutral density filter, flash exposure compensation or flash exposure lock.

■ If you don't get the colors you want, try different white balance settings. White balance can compensate for most lighting but when there is more than one light source, you may get color casts in your image. You'll have to experiment with this aspect, perhaps manually setting your own white balance if your camera has this feature. In other cases, you may find that you like the artificial colors or you may be able to adjust them in your photo-editing program.

PORTRAIT AND PRODUCT PHOTOGRAPHY—INTRODUCTION

Most photographers without studios use continuous lights that usually have three parts—stands, reflectors, and bulbs.

In the studio, you usually use more than one light to illuminate a portrait or product. The goal is often to create light that looks like that found outdoors. The lights can be hot lights, strobes, or slave flash units–or even fill cards. Sometimes you can get away with only one or two lights but the use of main, fill, background and rim lights is a classic studio lighting setup for portraits that can be adapted to other subjects.

■ **The main light** is positioned somewhat to one side of the subject and somewhat above it.

■ **A fill light** is placed opposite the main light, but more nearly at the subject's level.

■ **A background light** is used to control the lighting on the background behind the main subject.

■ **A rim light** is placed quite high and behind the subject to highlight edges and separate the subject from the background.

For most purposes you can get by with just the main light and a fill light. In fact, you can often get along with just the main light by replacing the fill light with reflectors to bounce light into the shadows. The way you position a light relative to the subject is very important.

■ As you move a light farther away from the subject you reduce the light falling on it. Because there is less light you may have to use a larger aperture which gives less depth of field.

■ Moving a light back hardens its light, while moving it closer softens it. By moving a light farther away, you also reduce the light it illuminates the subject with. On strobes, you do it by adjusting the light's intensity. On continuous lights you can do the same with a dimmer switch. You can have one light illuminate the subject with more intensity than another light. The difference between the two lights is called the *lighting ratio*.

■ Positioning the light at an angle to the subject will make the light uneven over the subject with the part closest to the light getting more light. The exposure will only be correct for those at one distance—normally those in the area metered by the autoexposure system. Parts of the setup located farther from the light source will be increasingly darker the farther away they are.

THE MAIN LIGHT

Outdoors the brightest source of light is usually the sun. In the studio, the sun's role is filled by the *main light*. Like the sun it's the brightest source of light and casts the darkest shadows.

Like the sun, the main light is often positioned above and slightly to the side of the subject. Placing the light above the subject creates light on the subject that is familiar, as are the shadows it creates.

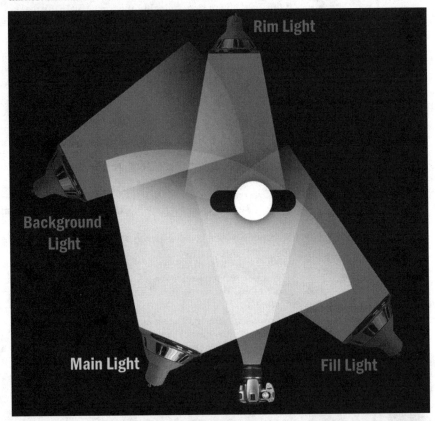

Here the main light is set to the left, above, and right of the subject.

FOR MORE ON TEXTBOOKS IN DIGITAL PHOTOGRAPHY, VISIT HTTP://WWW.PHOTOCOURSE.COM

THE FILL LIGHT

A fill light represents the light that falls on an outdoor subject from the broad expanse of an open sky, or reflecting from surfaces in the landscape. The fill light is almost always less bright than the main light, in fact about half as bright. Its relative brightness can be controlled in a number of ways. For example, it can be placed farther away from the subject, you can add a diffuser, or you can use a less powerful light.

The fill light, placed opposite the main light, opens shadows by lighting the dark side of the subject facing away from the main light.

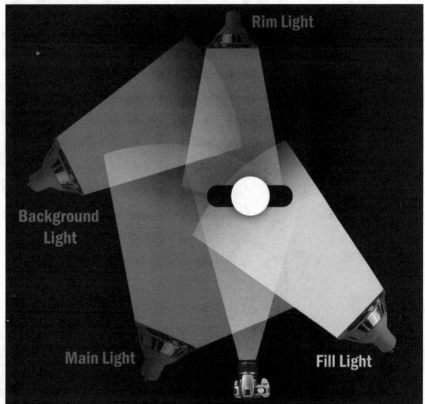

The fill light on the right of the subject is moved from close to the subject (left) to farther away (middle and right). The closer it is, the more it lightens shadows created by the main light.

THE BACKGROUND LIGHT

A background light controls how light or dark the background behind the subject is. A lighter or darker background can help visually separate the subject from the background. It can also lighten shadows cast on the background by other lights. In fact, if made bright enough, it can silhouette the subject.

The background light is off to the side and lights the background behind the subject without lighting the subject itself.

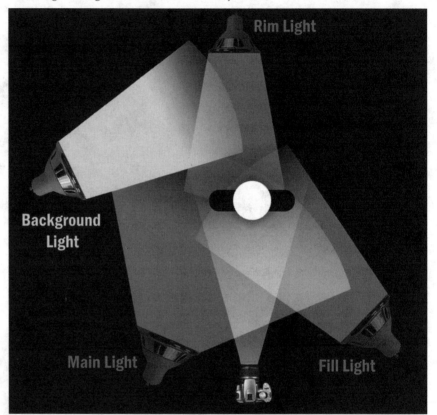

The background light can be varied for different effects. When only spillover light illuminates the background (far left) it's a uniform gray. When not illuminated at all (second from left) it's black. When the background is lit by a spot it is graduated (second from right). When illuminated with a bright light it is burned out to pure white (far right).

THE RIM LIGHT

A rim light positioned behind the subject and facing toward the camera illuminates the edges of the subject from behind so they glow and are visually separated from the darker background. In portrait photography a rim light is often used to back light the hair.

The rim light is often set up behind the subject and slightly higher than the other lights. Because this light is facing the camera, it's important that it be completely blocked by the subject or out of the field of view. If not you may get lens flare and lowered contrast. One way to block the light is to position a piece of cardboard (called a gobo) between the light and subject.

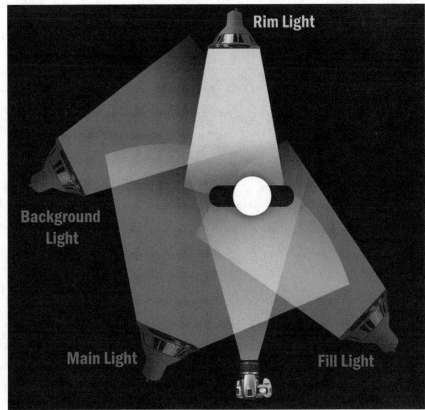

The final image is beautifully lit and well separated from the background. It's a visually interesting image.

Chapter 7
Exploring Special Features

CONTENTS
■ Shooting Panoramas■ Photographing in Black & White ■ Continuous Photography ■ Shooting Movies ■ Caring for Your Camera

D igital cameras offer a number of special features that offer exciting creative possibilities. These include the ability to take panoramas, capture images in black & white, and shoot a series of pictures instead of just one. Some digital cameras also let you capture short video clips, and some even capture it in TV quality. None of these features are difficult to use so you should give them a try. You'll find that they expand your range of creative tools and offer new opportunities for expressing ideas.

SHOOTING PANORAMAS

Although panoramic photographs have been taken in sections and pasted together for years, it was the development of digital photography and computer software that made seamless panoramas possible. To create a seamless panorama, you begin by capturing a series of overlapping images that you then combine seamlessly with a stitching program, one of which is often included with your camera or built into your photo-editing program.

The three images above have been stitched together into a single panorama (right).

There are a few important guidelines to follow for good panoramic images.

■ Zooming the lens to a wide angle requires fewer pictures to cover the same view but makes things appear smaller and more distant.

■ When photographing a horizontal or vertical sequence, stand in the same position and rotate the camera.

■ When photographing a document, center the camera over each section and keep it the same distance from the document for each shot.

■ Holding the camera vertically for horizontal panoramas gives you more height in the images but requires more images to cover the same horizontal area.

■ The camera should be as level as possible when you take the pictures. In a 360-degree pan, the first and last images must "connect" and overlap.

■ The images must overlap by 30-50% horizontally and not be out of vertical alignment by much more than 10%.

■ Avoid placing subjects that move in overlapping areas and don't combine nearby objects in the same scene as distant ones or they will be distorted.

■ Place a distinctive subject in each overlapping area to make it easy for the software to know how to combine the images.

The software you use to stitch images together can even out the lighting in a scene but it helps if you give it good images to work with. If your camera has an AE Lock feature, lock exposure for the entire series. Try to avoid extremes in lighting. These occur on bright sunny days when there are bright highlights and dark shadows. The problem is compounded because you may have to shoot into the sun. If you can pick your time, pick a day when it's cloudy bright—overcast but with slight shadows on the ground. If the sun is out, shoot at midday to keep the lighting even. If you have to shoot at other times, position the camera so direct sunlight is at your back, or if it has to be in front of you, try to block it with a tree or building. When shooting indoor panoramas, avoid shots of windows with direct sun shining through.

> **HOW TO: SHOOTING PANORAMAS**
> Look in your camera manual for a section on *panoramas*:
>
> _____
> _____
> _____
> _____
> _____
> _____
> _____
> _____
> _____
> _____
> _____

PHOTOGRAPHING IN BLACK AND WHITE

For years, photographers in the fine arts, perhaps the best known being Ansel Adams, have taken black and white pictures almost exclusively. If you want to work in the same medium, some cameras let you shoot in black and white as well as color. This mode is also useful if the photograph is going to be printed in black and white. If your camera doesn't have this mode, you can always make the conversion in your photo-editing program and then you'll have both a color and a B&W version.

One of the masters of black & white photography was Ansel Adams, shown here discussing his books with Tim Hill of New York Graphic Society.

On some digital cameras you can add an infrared filter and shoot black and white infrared images.

WHAT'S UP?

When taking pictures in black and white, they are displayed on the monitor in that format. This makes it much easier to visualize the end result. A film photographer has to do this visualization in his or her head.

HOW TO: SHOOTING IN BLACK & WHITE
Look in your camera guide for a section on *black and white, monochrome,* or *gray scale* photography:

_____

_____

_____

_____

CONTINUOUS PHOTOGRAPHY

The speed at which you can capture images in continuous mode is specified in frames per second (fps). This is usually between 3–5 fps.

With digital cameras, you normally take one photo at a time, but you're not limited to that way of shooting. You can also capture sequences of photos. In this continuous mode, you just hold down the shutter button and images are captured one after another until you release it. You can then choose the best image from the sequence or use all of them to create animations on your computer. The number you can capture is usually limited by the size of the camera's buffer. In some cases, the camera uses a smaller image size to capture sequences. This reduces the processing and storage time so you can take images at a faster rate.

Photo-editing programs often let you convert a series of images into an animated GIF. When posted on the Web, the images are quickly displayed one after the other like frames in a movie.

Continuous mode can capture a series of images much like movie frames. You can select the best one for printing, use them all to created an animation, or use the series to analyze an action such as the swing of a golf club or baseball bat.

Single and continuous mode icons.

HOW TO: USING CONTINUOUS PHOTOGRAPHY
Look in your camera guide for a section on *continuous, sequential,* or *multi-shot photography*:

_____

_____

_____

_____

SHOOTING MOVIES

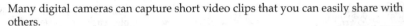

Movies can be played back on a computer equipped with the right software.

The almost universally recognized movie mode icon.

Many digital cameras can capture short video clips that you can easily share with others.

In most cases, image sizes are dramatically reduced from those used to capture still images. Sizes normally range from a very small 160 x 120 to a maximum of a TV quality 640 x 480 (VGA). The reason for this is so the camera can process the video as it's being captured and so file sizes are kept as small as possible.

Most digital cameras use AVI, MOV, or MPEG video formats so you can view or share them in a number of ways (if your video isn't in the "right" format, you can find programs that convert it):

■ **Your computer** can play back your movie as long as it's equipped with the appropriate software. This software comes with your camera, usually on a CD, but most new systems will also have it already installed.

■ **TV movies** have to be in MPEG format and on a Video CD or DVD disc. However, you can play back any format when you use a cable to connect your camera to the TV or VCR and use the camera as the playback device.

■ **E-mail** is a great way to distribute short video clips but anything longer than a few seconds may be too large to send. The recipient also has to have the necessary playback software installed to view the video.

■ **Web sites** are popping up all over that let you share movies with friends. You just upload your clip and send friends the location. When they visit the site that hosts your video, they can download or play it.

■ **iPods** and other portable devices play video clips in the formats they support.

Just playing back a video isn't all you can do with it. There are programs you can use to edit it or you can incorporate it into other larger projects. For example, you can insert movies into slide shows or even play them as wallpaper on your desktop. It's amazing how stringing together lots of very short clips can tell an interesting story.

Professional quality video is 30 fps but many cameras capture fewer than that.

Many digital cameras have a built in microphone that records sounds in movies or let's you attach sounds to images, perhaps to annotate them.

HOW TO: CAPTURING A MOVIE
Look in your camera guide for a section on *movie* or *video capture* or *record*:

_____

_____

HOW TO: PLAYING BACK A MOVIE
Look in your camera guide for a section on *movie* or *video play* or *playback*:

_____

_____

CARING FOR YOUR CAMERA

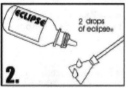

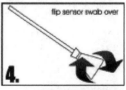

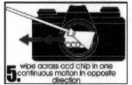

Here are the five steps recommended by Photographic Solutions for cleaning your image sensor with their sensor swabs and Eclipse cleaning fluid. http://www.photosol.com.

Some of the best opportunities for interesting photographs occur during bad weather or in hostile environments. You can take advantage of these opportunities as long as you take a few precautions to protect your camera.

CLEANING THE IMAGE SENSOR

When you change lenses on an SLR it's surprisingly easy to get dust on the image sensor that then shows up as dark spots in your images. One way to check if this has happened is to take a few photos of a clear sky or white card. Open the images in your photo-editing program and flip through them. (On a PC running PhotoImpact, zoom the pictures to the same size then Ctrl-Tab through them quickly and the dust spots jump out at you.) If all of the images have dark spots in the same place, that's dust on the sensor. To clean the sensor yourself you need more than courage. You also need sensor swabs and cleaning fluid. NEVER used compressed air, or other cleaning products, on the sensor. Cleaning supplies are available from B&H and Calumet. The most popular products seem to be those from Photographic Solutions (http://www.photosol.com). For more information Google "cleaning image sensor" but proceed at your own risk. One of the best Web sites I've found on this topic is *Cleaning Digital Cameras* at http://www.cleaningdigitalcameras.com/howto.html.

To clean a sensor you use the camera's command that locks the mirror up and out of the way and holds open the shutter so you can get to the surface of the image sensor. This is a high-risk procedure and we recommend extreme caution. It's more prudent to have it done by you camera company's service center.

CLEANING THE CAMERA AND LENS

Clean the outside of the camera with a slightly damp, soft, lint-free cloth. Open the "flaps" to the memory and battery compartments occasionally and use a soft brush or blower to remove dust. Clean the LCD monitor by brushing or blowing off dirt and wiping with a soft cloth, but don't press hard and be sure there is no grit on the cloth that can scratch the surface. Cleaning kits are available at most office supply stores.

The first rule is to clean the lens only when absolutely necessary. A little dust on the lens won't affect the image, so don't be compulsive. Keep the lens covered when not in use to reduce the amount of cleaning required. When cleaning is necessary, use a soft brush, such as a sable artist's brush, and a blower (an ear syringe makes a good one) to remove dust. Fingerprints can be very harmful to the lens coating and should be removed as soon as possible. Use a lens cleaning cloth (or roll up a piece of photographic lens cleaning tissue and tear the end off to leave a brush like surface). Put a small drop of lens cleaning fluid on the end of the tissue. (Your condensed breath on the lens also works well.) Never put cleaning fluid directly on the lens; it might run between the lens elements. Using a circular motion, clean the lens surface with the cloth or tissue, then use the cloth or a tissue rolled and torn the same way to dry. Never reuse tissues and don't press hard when cleaning because the front element of the lens is covered with a relatively delicate lens coating.

Blowing sand is one of the worst possible environments.

Use an umbrella or plastic bag to protect your camera from mist and light rain.

Protecting your Camera from the Elements

Your camera should never be exposed to excessively high temperatures. If at all possible, don't leave the camera in a car on a hot day, especially if the sun is shining on the car (or if it will later in the day). If the camera has to be exposed to the sun, such as when you are at the beach, cover it with a light colored and sand free towel or piece of tinfoil to shade it from the sun. Dark materials will only absorb the heat and possibly make things worse. Indoors, avoid storage near radiators or in other places likely to get hot or humid.

When it's cold out, keep the camera as warm as possible by keeping it under your coat. Always carry extra batteries. Those in your camera may weaken at low temperatures just as your car battery weakens in winter. Prevent condensation when taking the camera from a cold area to a warm one by wrapping the camera in a plastic bag or newspaper until its temperature climbs to match that of its environment. If some condensation does occur, do not use the camera or take it back out in the cold with condensation still on it or it can freeze up camera operation. Remove any batteries or flash cards and leave the compartment covers open until everything dries out.

Never place the camera near electric motors or other devices that have strong magnetic fields. These fields can corrupt the image data stored in the camera.

Always protect equipment from water, especially salt water, and from dust, dirt, and sand. A camera case helps but at the beach a plastic bag is even better. When shooting in the mist, fog, or rain, cover the camera with a plastic bag into which you've cut a hole for the lens to stick out. Use a rubber band to seal the bag around the lens. You can reach through the normal opening in the bag to operate the controls. Screwing a protective filter over the lens allows you to wipe off spray and condensation without damaging the delicate lens surface.

Protecting when Traveling

Use lens caps or covers to protect lenses. Store all small items and other accessories in cases and pack everything carefully so bangs and bumps won't cause them to hit each other. Be careful packing photographic equipment in soft luggage where it can be easily damaged. When flying, carry-on metal detectors are less damaging than the ones used to examine checked baggage. If in doubt, ask for hand inspection to reduce the possibility of X-ray induced damage.

Storing a Camera

Store cameras in a cool, dry, well ventilated area, and remove the batteries if they are to be stored for some time. A camera bag or case makes an excellent storage container to protect them from dust.

Digital cameras have lots of components including batteries, chargers, cables, lens cleaners, and what not. It helps if you have some kind of storage container in which to keep them all together.

Caring for Yourself

When hiking outdoors, don't wear the camera strap around your neck, it could strangle you. Don't aim the camera directly at the sun, it can burn the eye.